BROWN UNIVERSITY
A Short History

BY JANET M. PHILLIPS

Office of Public Affairs
and University Relations

Brown University

Design and typography: Kathryn de Boer
Printing: E.A. Johnson Company

ON THE COVER: *College Edifice and President's House. A colored reproduction, circa 1945, of the circa 1795 engraving by David Augustus Leonard.*

Office of Public Affairs and University Relations
Brown University
Providence, Rhode Island 02912
September 2000

❦ | *Contents*

🦋 Editor's Note

The first edition of this book, published in 1992, was so well received and proved useful to so many readers, it was clear to all involved in the project that someday it would need to be updated and reissued. That, indeed, has come to pass with the publication of this edition. But what the author, veteran Brown writer Janet M. Phillips '70, could not have foreseen was that the work of revising her manuscript would outlive Phillips herself.

Janet Phillips spent the first part of her career as a writer at the *Brown Alumni Monthly*, where in the 1970s and early 1980s she was a peerless copy editor and an author of award-winning articles. Several years ago, after completing revisions to two chapters of *A Short History* and writing a new section on the presidency of Vartan Gregorian, Phillips was diagnosed with cancer. She never got to see her revised history in print. On March 26, 2000, at the age of 50, she died at her home in Warwick, Rhode Island. For the many readers who admired this exceptional citizen of Brown, the new edition of *A Short History* will stand as a fitting memorial to Phillips's talents, her perseverance, and her love for her alma mater.

Anne Hinman Diffily '73

❧ | *Acknowledgments*

Nearly a decade has passed since the first edition of this book was written in 1991. Because the passage of time not only adds new chapters to a history, but affords new perspectives on earlier chapters, this second edition has been expanded and somewhat revised.

Many people who know and love Brown well have contributed to this project at various stages. Foremost among these are Eric Broudy, who as associate vice president for University relations patiently supervised the original project from start to finish, and Laura Freid, executive vice president for public affairs and University relations, who made updating this book a priority.

Special thanks are also due to Anne Diffily, former editor of the *Brown Alumni Magazine*, for her generosity with her notes and source materials; to Martha Mitchell and the staff of the University Archives for their encyclopedic knowledge of Brown; to John McIntyre, assistant to a half-dozen Brown presidents, who carefully read and critiqued the manuscripts; to the late Professor William McLoughlin, who read the original draft and clarified its picture of the historical context in which the University developed; and to Henry A.L. Brown of Warwick, a collateral descendant of Chancellor John Brown Francis (class of 1808), who gave me access to unpublished materials relating to the Brown and Francis families and their ties to the University. I am especially grateful to Vartan Gregorian, Brown's 16th president, whose generosity with his time and insights made easier the difficult task of gaining perspective on recent events.

Janet M. Phillips '70

A sampler "Wrought in the 10th Year
of her age" by Abigail Adams Hobart,
grandniece of President John Adams, in
1802. It depicts the College Edifice,
shown as "Providence College," and the
"President's House."

I | *Small Beginnings, Great Principles: A College for the Colony*

Colleges and universities with long histories, like Brown's, often possess an aura of timelessness, as if they had always been here and would always continue to be. It may be difficult to imagine any resemblance, past or present, between an Ivy League university with a 228-year history and a struggling new denominational college with a limited curriculum and even more limited resources. Yet Brown at its inception – and for many years afterward – was just that. Far from being "timeless," it was as timely as could be: Like most new ventures, it bore the unmistakable stamp of its era, its founders, and its place.

That era, of course, was the colonial one, and the Colony of Rhode Island and Providence Plantations was well into its second century before it finally acquired a college of its own. Roger Williams, fleeing Puritan religious oppression in Massachusetts Bay, founded Providence in 1636. Although he remained rigidly Calvinist in outlook all his life, Williams believed that no civil authority had the right to interfere with religious belief, and he made this the founding principle of his new settlement.

In due course Rhode Island attracted other like-minded individualists, some even more radical than Williams, and became famous – indeed, notorious – as a haven for unpopular religious minorities and unaffiliated "seekers." Walter Bronson, professor of English at Brown from 1892–1927 and author of the definitive *A History of Brown University*, summed it up pithily in that 1914 volume: "The afflicted and the eccentric from various quarters, Antinomians, Quakers, 'Seekers,' and Anabaptists of all stripes, had lived here together in tumultuous amity, attacking one another's heresies but steadily respecting everybody's right to preach heresy without any restraint from the civil power...."

'For the first time in human history,' writes the historian Richman, 'State had wholly been dissociated from Church in a commonwealth not utopian but real.' "

Inevitably, Rhode Island became fertile ground for the planting and cultivation of new varieties of religious belief, not merely for the transplanting of varieties that were persecuted elsewhere. Brown's "parent" denomination, the Baptist Church, was in its infancy in the 1630s, having been established only a quarter century earlier by English Separatists in Holland. It had no real foothold in the New World until Roger Williams became a convert to its beliefs. In 1638, just two years after his arrival in Rhode Island, he and a small group of followers founded the First Baptist Church in America. Only four months later, Roger Williams recanted *its* tenets, and he abstained from church membership ever after. But although the captain had jumped ship, the ship sailed on. The Providence congregation held together, and a new congregation was established in Newport in 1644.

The Baptist faith spread gradually through New England, the Middle Colonies (especially Pennsylvania and New Jersey), and the South – although, characteristically, as it grew it divided into schisms. Nevertheless, Baptists in general maintained a common sense of identity, and the faith continued to win converts. Unlike the Anglicans, Congregationalists (or Puritans), and Presbyterians – the more "established" Protestant churches, with their formal organization, their emphasis on the written Word, and their educated ministry – Baptism was a grass-roots inspirational religion. It distrusted and often despised ecclesiastical authority and anything that smacked of intellectualism. In a country where so many had fled from Old World authoritarianism, and where experience often carried more weight than book learning, it had a straightforward appeal to ordinary people. It was particularly well suited to the rebellious and egalitarian spirit of many

Rhode Islanders, who were much slower to embrace the mainline Protestant faiths.

Until the middle of the eighteenth century, those mainline churches were the keepers of the flame of higher education in the New World. The cerebral Puritans had wasted no time in founding Harvard, less than a decade after the Massachusetts Bay colony was settled, in 1636 (the same year Roger Williams paddled up the Seekonk River). The Anglicans established the College of William & Mary in Virginia in 1693; Yale, founded in 1701, gave New England a second Congregational stronghold. But these institutions were far from being the denominationally pure divinity schools they have often been stereotyped as. Although they were founded and controlled by religious bodies and tended to attract those of their own faith, none ever required students to belong to that faith. And although they did graduate large numbers of learned men for the ministry, they were part of a tradition of broader humanist scholarship in which their founders had been educated in Europe. As Richard Hofstadter notes, "The founding fathers of colonial education saw no difference between the basic education appropriate for a cleric and that appropriate for any other liberally educated man.... They intended their ministers to be educated side by side and in the same liberal curriculum with other civic leaders and men of affairs."

As the colonies in the eighteenth century became more settled (in every sense of the word) and prosperous, colonial life took on an increasing vigor, autonomy, and cosmopolitanism. America was coalescing as a society of its own making, not merely an offshoot of Europe. One of the byproducts of that process, and of the general rise in the standard of living, was a new consciousness about social standing. Americans living in a frontier society had almost prided themselves on being unsophisticated and unlettered; now they began to worry about respectability. This was especially true of middle-class Baptists, whose reputation for being an ignorant lot led by unlearned ministers made them squirm.

The eighteenth century also brought with it a phenomenon new in American life: a widespread religious revival that challenged the established churches and their theologies. The so-called Great Awakening of the 1730s and '40s dramatically divided the "Old Lights" (formal, doctrinaire) from the "New Lights" (inspirational, mystical). It swelled the ranks of sects like the Baptists, who absorbed various New Light factions that had split from their parent churches. And it provided an impetus for the founding of a new generation of colleges to train a new generation of ministers. Revivalist Presbyterians founded the College of New Jersey (Princeton) in 1746; and the Philadelphia Association of Baptists, having successfully launched a preparatory school in New Jersey in 1756, were soon emboldened to discuss plans for a college. Their search for a suitable locale led them straight to Rhode Island – the birthplace of their church – which had a large Baptist population and no college as yet.

Rhode Island, in turn, was ready to receive them. Ezra Stiles, a distinguished Congregationalist clergyman in Newport (and later president of Yale), had been planning a college for the state when the Baptists' emissary, James Manning, landed in Newport in July 1763. Manning's plan for a "liberal and catholic" institution, grounded in interdenominational cooperation, was readily endorsed by Rhode Island's leading citizens. Stiles and attorney William Ellery Jr. were asked to draw up a charter based on Manning's draft, which was then presented to the General Assembly. It divided the Corporation's power about equally among Baptists (who would make up a majority of the Trustees), Presbyterians and Congregationalists (either or both of whom –

The Rev. James Manning was the college's first president, as well as its first professor – of languages and "other Branches of Learning."

they were considered interchangeable – would be a majority of the Fellows), with a few slots reserved for Quakers and Anglicans and a few unallotted.

The Baptists, however, had second thoughts about the wisdom of this arrangement once the charter had been drawn up. Apparently they felt they had given away too much power, for a quarrel ensued with the Congregationalists that ended with the Baptists asserting definitive control over the college-to-be. Subsequent drafts of the charter placed the college presidency and a majority of the Fellows permanently in Baptist hands; they were given an even larger majority of the Trustees, and the Anglicans were promoted above the Congregationalists in number of allotted seats.

Sectarian squabbles aside, the charter was and is a distinguished document. The administrative reshuffling did not change its central intent nor its eloquent language, which remained, as

The 1914 Commencement ceremonies at the First Baptist Meeting House (at top) drew crowds of spectators, whether on foot or in more modern conveyances. Today (above), the scene is much the same, except for hair styles, dress, and vehicle.

Long before Rhode Island College became Brown University, its Commencement was the state's first public holiday. Although much of it was conducted in Latin or Greek and was over the audience's heads, it drew a large, mixed, and often boisterous crowd, the more respectable ones dressed to the nines and the rowdier ones ready to get drunk. (From 1790 onward, the sheriff of Providence County has attended every Commencement "to preserve the peace, good order, and decorum.") The *Providence Journal* suspended publication on Commencement Day well into the nineteenth century. Until the 1850s it was always held the first Wednesday in September; like Labor Day now, it officially marked the end of summer. In 1870 it was moved to June, but not until 1928 was it held on Mondays and preceded by a weekend of class and alumni activities. Since 1984 it's been held on Memorial Day weekend.

The early Commencements, which from 1776 on were held in the First Baptist Meeting House, required all graduates to have a speaking part – and the seniors were assessed fees in proportion to the magnitude of their parts, to pay for Commencement expenses. As public speaking gradually slipped from its central position in the Brown curriculum, the number of student orations was trimmed accordingly. Nevertheless, Brown has remained true to its tradition of having graduating seniors as the principal Commencement speakers, rather than invited dignitaries. The orations are still delivered in the First Baptist Church, but since 1947 the size of the graduating class (with attendant family, Corporation members, faculty, and guests) has required the degree-granting ceremonies to be held on the Green.

Commencement has twice been overshadowed by political events – first in 1775, when the seniors decided to cancel the ceremonies after the outbreak of war, and again in 1970, when the invasion of Cambodia and the killings at Kent State University triggered a nationwide student strike. Commencement wasn't canceled, but its format and content reflected the atmosphere of political crisis. Many seniors and faculty carried their mortarboards under their arms as a sign of protest on the march down College Hill, the ROTC commissioning ceremony was disrupted, Campus Dance was called off. A couple of innovations that year proved permanent: Senior Citations were awarded for the first time, and the weekend workshops and panels on hot political and social topics became today's Commencement Forums.

The Providence Journal *envisioned a campus teeming with "Gibson girls" and their escorts on Class Night in 1900.*

R.H. Ives Gammell's mural of the 1774 Commencement shows James Manning thanking Nicholas Brown and his brother Joseph for helping secure the college's new home in Providence.

Bronson notes, "almost wholly the work of Ezra Stiles." He saw the college's mission as one of preparing "a Succession of Men duly qualify'd for discharging the Offices of Life with usefulness and reputation" through instruction in "the Vernacular Learned Languages, and in the liberal Arts and Sciences." In providing that "Youths of all Religious Denominations shall and may be freely admitted to the Equal Advantages Emoluments & Honors of the College," and that "into this Liberal & Catholic Institution shall never be admitted any Religious Tests," the charter was not unusual for its day; other college charters had similar provisions. But it was unique in its declaration that "Sectarian differences of opinions shall not make any Part of the Public and Classical Instruction." And despite the Baptists' dominance, the charter, which was finally approved in March 1764, remained committed to the principle of denominational cooperation. "In so doing," Bronson writes, "it was true to the best traditions of the Baptist denomination and of the colony; and it was also wise after the manner of this world, by thus securing broader support than an institution controlled wholly by one sect could have won."

At the first meeting of the Corporation, held in September 1764 in Newport, twenty-four of the original incorporators were sworn in as members. They included such luminaries as the governor, Stephen Hopkins (later a signer of the Declaration of Independence), who was elected chancellor; his chief political rival, Samuel Ward, who also served several terms as governor; and Nicholas Brown Sr., one of the famous mercantile Brown brothers of Providence and father of Nicholas Brown, after whom the college was eventually named. The new institution, officially called Rhode Island College, had as yet no funds, no building, no students, and no faculty. So the Corporation's first order of business was to raise money, which it did by drawing up a list of sixty-nine persons around the country (including Benjamin Franklin) who were authorized to receive "subscriptions."

At its second meeting a year later, the Corporation named as president a man who had no serious rivals for the post: James Manning. Manning, anticipating the appointment, had settled in Rhode Island in 1764 as pastor of the new Baptist church in Warren, where he also opened a Latin school. His parsonage became the first home of Rhode Island College, which he served simultaneously as president and as professor of languages and "other Branches of Learning." The college already had a student: William Rogers, a precocious fourteen-year-old from Newport, who had matriculated the day before Manning's appointment and who was his sole college pupil for the next nine months.

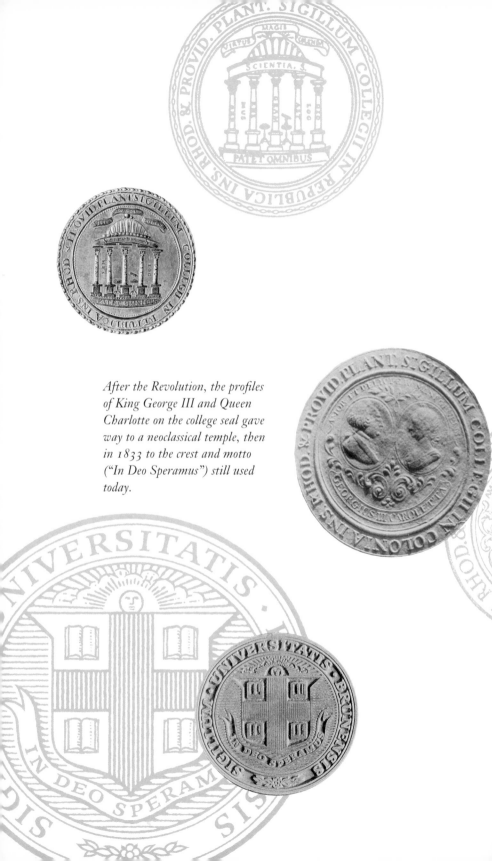

After the Revolution, the profiles of King George III and Queen Charlotte on the college seal gave way to a neoclassical temple, then in 1833 to the crest and motto ("In Deo Speramus") still used today.

2 | Breaking the Seal: Revolution and Independence

"A taste for Learning is greatly upon the increase in this Colony," James Manning remarked in 1766, soon after his brother-in-law, Richard Stites, had enrolled as Rhode Island College's second student. That taste was still not universal among Baptists, whose traditional prejudice against an educated and salaried ministry had sparked much debate in the ranks over the founding of their new college. But the college served a wider constituency, which unquestionably helped it survive those lean early years. The number of students increased steadily: Five more enrolled in 1766, another four in 1767, eight more in 1768 and eleven in 1769. Still, this was scarcely a flood, and tuition was so low ($12 a year) that operating funds had to be raised by other means.

In 1766 the Rev. Morgan Edwards was authorized to go to Europe and "solicit Benefactions for this Institution." (That Europe was the first choice as a source of donations shows the extent to which the New World was still an appendage of the Old – despite the arduousness of trans-Atlantic travel and the difficulties of communication in those days.) During a year and a half in Great Britain and Ireland, he raised the equivalent of $4,300, including donations from the likes of Benjamin Franklin and Thomas Penn, who gave $50 or $100 apiece. The donors, of various Protestant persuasions, willingly supported the cause of education in general and of "this Liberal & Catholic Institution" in particular. Edwards's subscription book, as Walter Bronson notes, contains "on the same time-stained pages the names of obscure men and women...who out of their poverty gave their one shilling or two shillings sixpence to aid the cause of education in a distant college from which they could never

Completion of the College Edifice was delayed by the Revolution: The first two floors were finished and occupied by 1771–72, the third floor in 1785, and the fourth in 1788. The French troops quartered there during the war almost succeeded in dismantling it; luckily, their plan to strip and sell its boards was averted at the last minute. But generations of service as a dormitory nearly doomed it again in the 19th century, when it was rescued and renovated into offices.

expect to receive any personal benefit." After Edwards returned, the Rev. Hezekiah Smith was sent on a similar expedition to the Southern colonies, raising another $1,700.

The college was still operating out of Manning's parsonage in Warren when it held its first Commencement in September 1769. That first graduating class had only seven students, but the ceremonies lasted all day and into the evening – and are of special interest for what they reflected of the prevailing political weather. They featured a vigorous debate on the thesis, "The Americans, in their present Circumstances, cannot, consistent with good Policy, affect to become an independent State." The *Newport Mercury*, in its account of the day's festivities, tactfully declined to say who lost the debate, but it pointedly noted that "the President and all the Candidates were dressed in American Manufactures." (Harvard's graduating class had made the same gesture the previous year.)

Whatever political storms were gathering on the horizon, the Corporation had more immediate and pressing concerns. Chief among these was choosing a permanent home for the college, and on that first Commencement Day it decided in favor of Bris-

tol County, Warren's location. No further debate or discussion seemed necessary – until word of the choice got around the colony. East Greenwich, Providence, and Newport all protested hotly, each proclaiming its superior qualifications to be the colony's seat of higher education. The Corporation retracted its decision, and the contest quickly narrowed to Providence and Newport; Newport was the larger and richer of the two, but Providence had powerful allies in Manning himself and the Brown family, as well as other arguments in its favor. The colony had its origin there, as did the Baptist Church in America, and its economic vigor boded well for its future. When the Corporation settled on Providence in February 1770, Newport's partisans, in a fit of pique, took steps to charter a rival college in their home town. But the Corporation's protests to the General Assembly quashed the idea, and no more was heard of it.

A few months later the college's president, its first tutor

The destiny of Nicholas Brown Jr. and that of Rhode Island College were so intertwined that it seems almost inconceivable in retrospect that Brown University might have been named for anyone else. Nicholas graduated from the college in 1786 at age seventeen, and by age twenty-two was already a trustee. He just as quickly assumed a leading role in Providence's (and Rhode Island's) economic life by establishing the firm of Brown & Ives, which became one of New England's largest mercantile houses. His benefactions to Brown, totaling $160,000 over his lifetime, sprang partly from a sense of proprietorship that his family passed to him, and partly from his own generosity of temperament and broad vision. Francis Wayland said of him, "He was endowed to an unusual degree with that quality, which I know not how better to express than by the term, largeness of mind. A plan or an enterprise was attractive to him, all things being equal, in proportion to its extensiveness." According to Wayland, he had a large heart as well, full of "active sympathy for every form of human suffering. He not infrequently visited the sick in their own dwellings, while his door was frequently thronged, and his steps waylaid by the poor and unfortunate of every age." He served continuously as a trustee and then a fellow of the University until his death in 1841; he also helped found Butler Hospital, the state's first mental hospital, and the Providence Athenaeum.

(David Howell), and its students took up residence at various private houses in Providence. Classes were held in the brick schoolhouse at the west end of Meeting Street, amid the congestion and noise of downtown. The Corporation had been scouting for a building site in the "regions calm of mild and serene air" at the top of what is now College Hill, "above the smoke & stir of this dim spot." Of the eight-acre site it purchased (partly from John and Moses Brown), which commanded a broad view of the town below, of Narragansett Bay and miles of gently rolling farmland and woodland, Morgan Edwards remarked, "Surely this spot was made for a seat of the Muses!"

No time was lost in putting a roof over the Muses' heads: In May of 1770 the cornerstone of the College Edifice, now University Hall, was laid. The plans were modeled on Nassau Hall at Princeton, the alma mater of both Manning and Howell. Nicholas Brown and Company, the Brown brothers' firm, had charge of the construction, which progressed with remarkable efficiency. This may have been partly due to their willingness to motivate the crew with generous supplies of rum punch. John Brown's meticulous account book shows the expenditures at each stage of building, e.g.: "To 2 Galls. W.I. [West Indian] Rum 7s. 2 lbs Sugar 1s. when Laying the 2d floor." By the winter of 1771–72, the four-story structure was closed in and the first two floors ready for occupancy. A house for the president had also been built just northwest of the College Edifice. The *Boston Gazette* twitted the Corporation for building "a College near as large as Babel; sufficient to contain ten Times the Number of Students" that could ever be expected to enroll. Time, of course, stood that prophecy on its head; meanwhile, the college's officers and its twenty-one students could be excused for the pride they took in their spacious new quarters.

The college was finally beginning to take on what Bronson

PROVIDENCE 1790

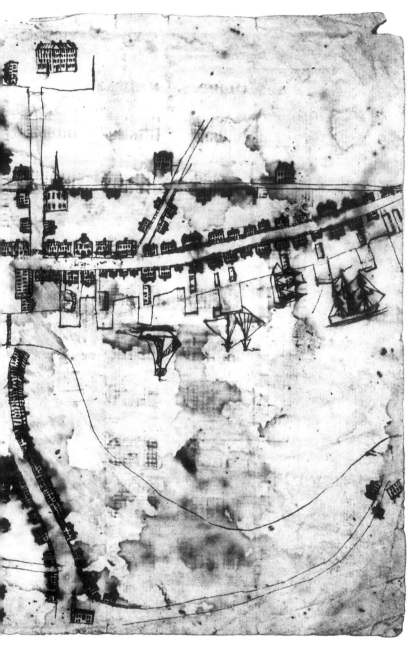

*This bird's-eye view of Providence, with the College Edifice
and the president's house at the top, was drawn by John Fitch
in 1790 when he was a student at Rhode Island College.*

calls a "settled air" just as the political climate was becoming radically unsettled. The Sugar Act of 1764, the Stamp Act of 1765, the Declaratory Act of 1766, the Townshend Acts of 1767, and the Tea Act of 1773 were experienced in the colonies as a sort of drum roll of mounting British tyranny. And Rhode Island, obstreperous as ever, "rushed pell-mell toward revolution after 1764," in the words of William McLoughlin: "the first colony to resort to armed resistance, to call for a Continental Congress, to renounce allegiance to the king, to create an American naval force." The college's Commencement programs from the early 1770s reflect a growing preoccupation with the colonies' fate, and the Class of 1775 decided to forgo the festivities of a public

Commencement, in sober recognition of "the Distresses of our oppressed Country, which now most unjustly feels the baneful Effects of arbitrary Power." The last Commencement until after the Revolution was held in 1776 in the newly completed First Baptist Church; that year the college awarded an honorary Master of Arts degree to Gen. Nathanael Greene,

THIS is to inform all the Students, that their Attendance on College Orders is hereby dispensed with, until the End of the next Spring Vacation; and that they are at Liberty to return Home, or profecute their Studies elfewhere, as they think proper: And that thofe who pay as particular Attention to their Studies as thefe confufed Times will admit, fhall then be confidered in the fame Light and Standing as if they had given the ufual Attendance here. In Witnefs whereof, I fubfcribe

JAMES MANNING, Prefident.

Providence, December 10.

President Manning published this notice in the Providence Gazette *in December 1776. The college didn't reopen until 1782.*

the commander of the state's armed forces, who was soon to become a Revolutionary hero.

Once war broke out, it was only a question of time before the college would be forced to shut down. That time came in December 1776, when the British seized Newport and Aquidneck Island. "This brought their Camp in plain View from the

The 18th-century Spanish chair that Brown presidents sit in while conferring degrees was booty from a captured Spanish vessel bound for the West Indies. Benjamin Wicker presented the chair to his friend Stephen Hopkins, governor of Rhode Island (1758–68) and the first chancellor of Rhode Island College, and in 1848 Stephen Hopkins Smith made a gift of it to President Wayland.

College with the naked Eye," Manning wrote, "upon which the Country flew to Arms & marched for Providence." The College Edifice was seized for use as a barracks, and the students turned out. Immediately afterward, Manning published a notice in the *Providence Gazette* dismissing the students until the following spring. But things were no better in May of 1777, when he published another notice acknowledging that the college could not reopen "while this continues a garrisoned Town." The current senior class received their degrees at a meeting of the Corporation in September, the last business the college transacted until 1780.

Manning was by no means at loose ends without a college to preside over. He had assumed the pastorate of the Baptist Church in Providence after leaving Warren, and he worked tirelessly, through many channels, to relieve the widespread hunger and distress war brought to Rhode Island. In 1777 he finished building thirty-two rods of stone wall on the college land with his own hands. From 1778 onward he joined forces with Moses Brown and Stephen Hopkins in agitating for the abolition of slavery and slave trading in the state. (Manning had freed his only slave in 1770.) But his first commitment was to the college, and within eight days after the American troops vacated it in

The college's first chancellor, Stephen Hopkins (1707–1785), was also a three-term governor of the colony, a signer of the Declaration of Independence, and a delegate to the Continental Congress.

April 1780, he had presented to the Corporation a proposal for reopening it in May. What Bronson aptly calls "this courageous beginning amidst the ruin left by war" was short-lived: On June 5, Manning was informed by Gov. William Greene II that the College Edifice was again to be commandeered for military use, this time as a hospital for French troops.

In the ensuing two years, Manning tutored several students under his own roof, enabling them to receive their bachelor's degrees in 1782. When the French troops finally cleared out of the College Edifice in May of that year (but not before they had tried to strip the building of its boards and windows to sell them), the "ruin left by war" was a literal description of its condition. Manning referred to it as the "Augean Stable." The Corporation promptly submitted a bill for the equivalent of $4,400 to the new federal government, asking recompense for use and damages from 1776 onward. Eighteen years later, the college was reimbursed $2,779.13 for its occupancy by American troops alone.

At the Corporation's first postwar meeting in September 1782, one of its first orders of business was to break the old college seal, with its profiles of King George and Queen Charlotte,

HORACE MANN
CLASS OF 1819

The opportunity to carry out his life's work in public education came to Horace Mann, class of 1819, quite by surprise. After graduating from Brown, he made a distinguished name for himself as a lawyer in Boston and was elected first to the Massachusetts House, then the Senate. He had solid reformist credentials, but had never gotten deeply involved in public education until he cast his vote in 1837 in favor of creating the nation's first State Board of Education. It was expected that James G. Carter, who had worked almost single-handedly for years to improve public schools in Massachusetts, would become the board's first secretary. Instead, the board surprised everyone and chose Horace Mann. Awed by the immensity of the challenge, Mann swore to himself the day he accepted, "Henceforth, as long as I hold this office, I dedicate myself to the supremest welfare of mankind upon earth." Over the next twelve years he transformed the state's hodgepodge of common schools (basically charity schools for the poor) into a great system of free public schools, organized on solid educational principles. And he accomplished this feat by persuasion alone, for the board had no power to compel or enforce anything. Mann held teachers' institutes and public meetings in every county, using the oratorical skills he had honed at Brown, to raise public con-sciousness (which he likened to "trying to batter down Gibraltar with one's fist"). His twelve annual reports to the board still stand as a monument of educational thought. In 1848 Mann was elected to Congress to fill the seat vacated by John Quincy Adams's death, where he fought vigorously against slavery; in 1854 he was named president of Antioch College in Ohio, and served out his days there. His statue and that of Daniel Webster still flank the entrance to the Massachusetts State House.

❦ SAMUEL GRIDLEY HOWE, M.D.
CLASS OF 1821

Samuel Gridley Howe, M.D., class of 1821, is memorialized both on the walls of the Boston Public Library and in a street that bears his name in Athens, Greece. Like his contemporary, Horace Mann, Howe embodied those nineteenth-century reformist sympathies that strove to abolish slavery and all forms of institutionalized mistreatment or neglect – in such places as prisons, schools, and insane asylums. Like another contempo-

rary, Lord Byron, he was stirred by the Greek revolution against the Ottoman Turks. In 1824, shortly after earning his M.D. from Harvard, he sailed for Greece to volunteer as a soldier and surgeon in the war, and was eventually made surgeon-in-chief to the Greek navy. Returning to Boston, he helped establish the New England (later Perkins) Institution for the Blind and became a virtually self-taught pioneer in educating the blind. He worked with Horace Mann on behalf of public education in Massachusetts, and lobbied for the mentally ill, the retarded, and prisoners. He and his wife, Julia Ward Howe (author of "The Battle Hymn of the Republic" and first president of the New England Woman Suffrage Association), edited the anti-slavery paper *The Commonwealth*, helped rescue fugitive slaves, and raised money to keep Kansas a Free Soil state. Ironically, Howe was best known at Brown for his pranks (putting hot ashes in a tutor's bed, leading the president's horse to the top floor of University Hall), which it still amused him to recount years later. As his daughter Laura observed, "The very ardor of temperament which led him on from scrape to scrape was that which later was to carry him through fire and water" both at home and abroad.

and commission a new one. Alterations to the charter were made to reflect the shift from colonial status; a new tutor was appointed (David Howell by then was a delegate to the Continental Congress); and the college's books and papers, which had been taken elsewhere for safekeeping, were returned to campus. But amid the general destitution and disarray of the immediate postwar period, funds and students – the most necessary items of all – were scarce indeed. After casting about for a viable fundraising strategy, the Corporation came up with a novel idea: to appeal to the King of France.

This scheme was not as outlandish as it might sound. Britain was obviously not the place to seek funds then, and France had been an ally (and a house guest) during the Revolution. In addition, the king had reportedly offered aid to Yale and had been declined. So an address was drawn up and forwarded to Benjamin Franklin, minister at the French court. He apparently took no action, and two years later, in 1786, the Corporation renewed its request through Thomas Jefferson, the new minister to France. Jefferson tactfully informed Corporation members that his preliminary inquiries had met with no encouragement, and the matter was dropped.

The college did have one windfall during this period: In 1783, John Brown offered to pay half the cost of a "compleat Philosophical Apparatus and Library," and the Corporation promptly raised the other half. (The term "philosophical apparatus" referred to the instruments – telescopes, microscopes, globes, magnets, etc. – used in studying the natural sciences, which in those days went under the heading of "natural philosophy.") The acquisition of these sorely needed books and equipment put the college on a more solid academic footing, and it began to attract more students, which in turn meant more revenue. But the money's arrival was slow and often sporadic – many students

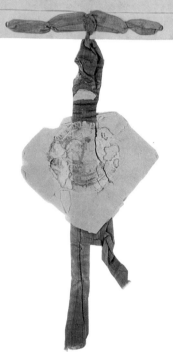

William Williams received this diploma at the college's first Commencement in 1769.

were in arrears on tuition and fees – and the college's poverty almost cost it its president.

By the winter of 1786–87, the normally cheerful and resilient Manning was near the end of his rope. He had recently been pressed into serving seven months in the U.S. Congress, but had yet to be paid for it; and the arrearages of tuition at the college meant that he had been unable to collect his salary. Broke, ill, and weary, he wrote to a friend that he was seriously considering leaving Rhode Island; and in his uncharacteristically black mood, he suspected Howell of plotting to unseat him because Howell had openly disagreed with him on a matter of student discipline. However, as his health and his finances improved, Manning regained his composure.

The first post-Revolutionary Commencement was held in 1786, when a class of fifteen (including Nicholas Brown Jr.) was awarded degrees. The trials of new nationhood were hinted at by one of the debate topics: "Whether it would not have been better for America to have remained dependent on Great Britain." By then, Commencement had become the town's first public holiday, whose high spirits sometimes spilled over into rowdiness. The Corporation tried to lessen the carnival atmosphere by pressuring the Baptist Society in 1790 to crack down on "the erection of Booths, or receptacles for liquors, or other things for sale" on the grounds of the Meeting House. That year's Commencement was a watershed of sorts: It was the largest to date (twenty-two graduated); it was held not long after Rhode Island became the last state to ratify the Constitution; and it conferred an honorary degree on George Washington, who had visited the state a few weeks earlier to give the newest member of the Union his blessings. That Commencement was also the last at which Manning presided. He died of a stroke on July 24, 1791, at the age of fifty-two.

View of the East Side and College Hill painted
for the drop curtain at the Providence Theater
by noted Boston artist John Worrall.

3 | Old Systems and New: The Search for Identity

The man who took James Manning's place at the helm of Rhode Island College was younger even than the college itself. The Rev. Jonathan Maxcy, class of 1787, was only twenty-four when he was named president *pro tem* in 1792. He had served as a tutor since his graduation, had succeeded Manning as pastor of the First Baptist Church, and had recently been made professor of divinity; he was called to the presidency after the Corporation's first choice, Dr. Samuel Jones of Pennsylvania, declined because of advancing age. Maxcy was probably the youngest college president in the country at the time of his appointment, and the Corporation thought it wise to keep him on *pro tem* status for five years, after which he "graduated" to president.

The college he took over had quadrupled its enrollment in the past two decades: By 1793–94, there were eighty-three undergraduates, most of them from Massachusetts, Rhode Island, and Connecticut. Their course of study was based on the venerable triad of classics, mathematics, and metaphysics, with the addition of English grammar and rhetoric, and of a few scientific and practical subjects such as astronomy, geography, surveying, and navigation. There were no electives, and no concentrations: The curriculum was the same for all. The dawn of academic specialization was still a generation or two away.

Students lived, ate, studied, and worshiped in the College Edifice (nicknamed the "Old Brick"), under the vigilant eyes of the tutors and steward, who were required to live there as well, and often of their professors, who were encouraged to do the same. The president's house was next door, so he too was omnipresent. This was the "family model" of undergraduate life, adapted from Oxford and Cambridge, and the concept of *in loco parentis* was applied quite literally. Indeed, most students probably lived under stricter discipline at college than at home: Approximately ten hours a day were designated study hours, during which students had to remain alone in their rooms, and attendance at morning and evening prayers was mandatory.

Jonathan Maxcy, class of 1787, was twenty-four years old when he succeeded James Manning as President.

Youth, as always, chafed at the bit. The college records from 1791 note that "Fairbanks is fined also 6/ for permitting, some time since, liquor to be brought into, and to be drunk in his room.... Howell [is] fined 6/ for...at late Hours in the night running through the College, beating against the doors, hallooing and using prophane [sic] language." A student's letter of 1799 notes, "The Old Brick resounds very frequently with the breaking of glass bottles against Tutor T's door, If he can be called a Tutor. We have given him the epithet of Weazle." Punishments ran the gamut from fines to public rebuke to "rustication" (temporarily banishing a student to some rural pastor's house) to – rarely – expulsion. The college's historians seem to agree that the campus was a bit rowdier under Maxcy's administration, perhaps because his youth failed to intimidate students.

Maxcy nonetheless did much to increase the college's reputation. He was a brilliant orator in an era when that skill was considered of preeminent importance, and Rhode Island College became known for its teaching of oratory and belles-lettres. Its enrollment continued to grow, but not its operating funds. In 1795 the Corporation tried a new tactic, one that had succeeded at other colleges: It voted that "any person giving to this Corporation the sum of Six thousand dollars, or good security therefor,

Brown University Glee Club.

The late 19th-century yearbooks were brightened with lighthearted cartoons. This one is from the 1886 Liber Brunensis.

Undergraduate literary life at Brown made its debut in 1829 with *The Brunonian,* a more-or-less-monthly periodical that printed student essays, Commencement orations, poems, and such. In mid-century it was followed by the more factual *Brown Paper* (1857–68), an organ of the Greek-letter societies that published lists of their members, items of college news, and editorials. (Not entirely factual, though: James DeWolf's lyrics to "Alma Mater" first appeared in the 1860 edition of the *Brown Paper.*) When the *Brown Paper* became the *Liber Brunensis* in 1868, the *Brunonian* was revived, and flourished for another half century (until 1917). By then, Brown had a full-fledged campus newspaper – the *Brown Daily Herald,* founded in 1891 – and an alumni magazine, the *Brown Alumni Monthly,* which since its inception in 1900 has developed into one of the best university magazines in the country. During the heyday of college humor magazines in the '20s, the *Brown Jug* poured out wit and satire from the likes of S.J. Perelman, class of 1925.

Today, word processors and desktop printers have given birth to any number of campus publications: The more established ones include *Issues Monthly, Journal of the Arts, Mediatribe, Passion Fruit Review,* and the *College Hill Independent.*

The Brunonian, *launched in 1829, was Brown's first literary magazine. Its successor, the* Brown Paper, *published James DeWolf's lyrics for "Alma Mater."*

before the next annual Commencement, shall have the honour of naming this University."

No suitor was forthcoming, so the college had to retain its maiden name for a few more years. Meanwhile, Maxcy resigned in 1802 to accept the presidency of Union College in Schenectady, and the Corporation chose a new president from the ranks of the faculty. Asa Messer, professor of mathematics and natural philosophy, was a comparatively ripe thirty-three years old and had already served on the faculty eleven years. After his election, the Corporation tried again to find a patron, this time offering slightly easier terms: It voted in 1803 that a donation of $5,000 would entitle the donor to name the college.

This time a suitor did come forward, an alumnus and old friend of the college. Nicholas Brown's gift of $5,000 to endow a chair in oratory carried out the wishes of his recently deceased uncle, John Brown, and was the first in a series of increasingly liberal gifts over his lifetime. Later generations have sometimes jokingly accused him of buying fame cheap with that $5,000, but that was a substantial sum in those days, and by contemporary accounts Brown appears to have been a true *rara avis* – a wealthy and prominent man who was both generous and modest. In September 1804, at the same meeting in which the gift was announced, the Corporation voted to change the college's name to "Brown University in Providence in the State of Rhode Island, and Providence Plantations."

The newly christened university branched out in 1811 by establishing a medical school, or at least the beginnings of one. Three well-known physicians (Solomon Drowne, William Ingalls, and William C. Bowen) were appointed as lecturers on medical subjects – albeit without the aid of textbooks, laboratories, equipment or endowment. Walter Bronson points out that even by the standards of that era, when medicine, like most professions, was learned primarily through apprenticeship and not academic preparation, Brown's medical school had a long way to go. After some prodding, additional faculty were appointed to fill gaps in the curriculum. The professors appear to have taken responsibility for providing the necessary supplies: One Professor Parsons made secret and not entirely legal arrangements to procure a stock of "anatomical material," according to his son. In any case, the medical school flourished – thanks largely to its distinguished faculty – and became a credit to the University while it lasted.

The other great addition in President Messer's tenure was a new college building. The "Old Brick" was bulging at the seams

John Hay, class of 1858, showed literary promise from a young age and was chosen class poet during his senior year at Brown. But on returning home to Warsaw, Ill., he found few prospects for a career in letters in what he called "this barbarous West." In 1859 he reluctantly joined his uncle's law office in Springfield. Next door was the office of Abraham Lincoln. When Lincoln was elected in 1860, Hay and a friend, John Nicolay, accompanied him to Washington as private secretaries. Hay's companionship with the President (whom he fondly nicknamed the "Ancient" and the "Tycoon") left him with an intimate and abiding sense of Lincoln's greatness. He and Nicolay often discussed the possibility of writing a book about those momentous years, but the project had to wait. Hay was appointed secretary to the American legation in Paris in March 1865, the first of several diplomatic posts in Europe. On returning to the States in 1870, he had a brief fling with journalism, then launched his literary career with *Pike County Ballads and Other Pieces*, *Castilian Days*, and his collected *Poems*. In 1875 he and Nicolay began the collaboration that resulted, 15 years later, in the publication of the ten-volume *Abraham Lincoln: A History*. It was their monument to the President they had served,

This unusual painted photograph of President Lincoln with his secretaries, John Hay (standing) and John Nicolay, is from the Lincoln collection at the John Hay Library.

and it remains an invaluable historical record based on original sources (much of it material loaned by Lincoln's son Robert). Hay had returned to public life as assistant secretary of state in 1878 under Rutherford B. Hayes; after the Lincoln opus was published, he became an adviser to President William McKinley, ambassador to Great Britain in 1897, and finally secretary of state from 1898–1905 under McKinley and Teddy Roosevelt. Hay's name is primarily linked with the "Open Door" policy in China, but his greatest success there may have been to prevent the Chinese empire from breaking up in the Boxer Rebellion of 1900. Under Roosevelt, he also settled the Alaskan boundary dispute with Canada and was a key player in the creation of the Panama Canal.

by 1821, when the Corporation decided to purchase an adjacent lot from Nathan Waterman. Nicholas Brown again stepped forward and paid the entire cost of a new three-story brick building, which he named Hope College after his sister. On its completion in 1823, the old College Edifice was duly renamed University Hall, a fence was put up around the grounds, and trees planted – the beginnings of a real college campus.

Despite the considerable strides made during his administration and the generally high personal regard in which he was held, Messer's presidency came to an unhappy end. By the 1820s, a new and heretical faith called Unitarianism was spreading rapidly, and sects like the Baptists that had once been in the vanguard of heresy now felt themselves threatened, like any establishment church, by new waves of dissent. Messer was suspected by some Corporation members of being a fellow traveler of the Unitarians, and he was repeatedly challenged on his belief in the divinity of Christ. He defended himself against this "Spanish Inquisition" (his words), but when anonymous pamphlets attacking him began to circulate, and Corporation members began citing them in meetings, Messer resigned in bitterness and disgust. He clearly, and understandably, felt betrayed by the institution to which he had devoted thirty-nine years of his life, twenty-four of them as president.

On the same day it accepted Messer's resignation in 1826, the Corporation named as his successor a man who was to transform Brown profoundly. Francis Wayland, age thirty-one, professor of mathematics and natural philosophy at Union College, had started out to study medicine, then found his true calling in the ministry; he was already a leading figure among Baptists when he was named a Fellow of Brown University in 1825. Wayland was a forceful personality with strong views, and on taking office in 1827 he immediately embarked on a vigorous intellectual and moral housecleaning. Academic and disciplinary standards were tightened, entrance requirements were raised, and student pastimes that Wayland considered frivolous (like singing in one's room) were squelched. There were murmurs of protest, but most seemed to welcome this invigorating new wind that blew across campus.

Wayland's next move, however, was far more controversial. He was an earnest believer in the "family model" of the college community and in close supervision of campus life. By those lights, he concluded that non-resident professors, like those in the medical school, did not belong at Brown. Within a month of assuming office, he persuaded the Corporation to fire them indirectly by cutting off their salaries and fees – all except Professor Bowen, who was also the librarian. Brown thus lost not only its medical school, but another star faculty member: Tristram Burges, who had been named in 1815 to the chair in oratory endowed by Nicholas Brown. A storm of protest broke out on campus and in the community; angry editorials and letters to the editor appeared in the local papers, some suggesting that the time was ripe for another college in Rhode Island, one organized on more democratic principles. But Wayland simply ignored his critics, and the protests died out.

The call for another college in the state "to furnish a broader and more practical education," although it would be fifty years before it was realized, was prophetic of the enormous social changes that were beginning to press in on Brown and other colleges. The Industrial Revolution was well under way (nowhere more so than in Rhode Island); great strides were being made in technology and science; and America, after the War of 1812, had a new sense of national identity and an obsession with westward expansion. The tide of progress was moving ever faster, and those who did not move with it would simply be left stranded.

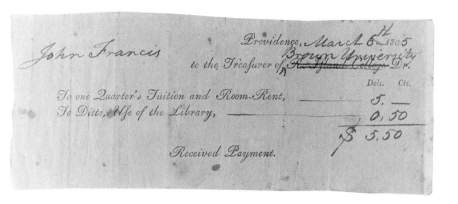

John Brown Francis's 1805 receipt for tuition, room rent, and use of the library reflects the college's new identity as Brown University. Francis (class of 1808) served as chancellor from 1841 to 1854.

Wayland was not blind to these larger issues or their implications for higher education. He took steps early on to broaden the curriculum and bring it more in line with the times, adding courses such as chemistry, physiology, political economy, French and Hebrew, and calculus. Students were even allowed a limited choice of electives. But there were urgent practical needs at Brown that had to be addressed before any sweeping changes in educational philosophy could be considered. The library, for one, was understocked and underfunded. In 1831 the Corporation authorized a subscription for the unprecedented sum of $25,000 to set up a permanent library fund. Wayland spearheaded the drive and succeeded in raising more than $19,000 ($10,000 from Nicholas Brown, the rest from many other donors), which was put at interest until it grew to $25,000. Next, the library needed new quarters; Nicholas Brown contributed $18,500 to build Manning Hall, which housed the library downstairs and the chapel upstairs. Four years later, in 1839, the sciences acquired a new home in Rhode Island Hall, for which Nicholas Brown gave the land and most of the funds.

As the University's intellectual life was recharged and its

Inman Page, class of 1877, the first
African-American to graduate from
Brown, was born into slavery in 1853.
He was a ten-year-old houseboy on a
Virginia plantation when he and his
family escaped through the nearby battle lines in 1863 and fled to Washington. Fourteen years later, he was chosen
class orator at Brown's Class Day – not,
as the *Providence Journal*
observed, out of a sense
of chivalry, but because
he was "an orator of rare
ability" in a college that prided itself on
the eloquence of its graduates. After a
year of teaching at Natchez Seminary in
Mississippi (as Reconstruction was being
dismantled in the South), Page joined
the faculty of Lincoln Institute in Jefferson City, Mo. Much of the rest of his
life was dedicated, as Ralph Ellison has
noted, to implanting the New England
tradition of education in the newer states
out West – transmitting that tradition
to former slaves and their children and
grandchildren. Page served as president
of Lincoln Institute (later Lincoln University), Langston University in Oklahoma, Western Baptist College in Macon,
Mo., and Roger Williams University
in Nashville. After the First World War,
he devoted most of his remaining years
(he died in 1935) to serving as principal
and supervisor of Oklahoma City's black
public schools.

material wants were met, extracurricular life began to flourish. The first college magazine, *The Brunonian*, was founded in 1829; a Phi Beta Kappa chapter was established in 1830; fraternities took hold in the late 1830s, despite Wayland's initial suspicions about them; and the first general alumni association was founded in 1842. (There were still no organized sports at Brown, the principal form of exercise being "to promenade on the north side of Westminster Street after 5 P.M.," as one student put it.)

But Wayland was not inclined to be complacent. On sabbatical in Europe in 1840–41, he spent most of his time visiting British universities and meeting with leading scholars and intellectuals. He was brimming with ideas when he returned, which he put into a report to the Corporation in 1841 and into a book entitled *Thoughts on the Present Collegiate System in the United States* in 1842. The core of his proposal was that colleges should "adapt their courses to the different capacities and wants of students" – in short, adjust themselves to the realities of a varied and competitive American market, and give the public what it seemed to demand.

As in Revolutionary days, though, outside events suddenly intruded and put academic matters on the back burner. The Dorr Rebellion of 1842 was the climax of a struggle over voting rights and legislative representation. In 1840, Rhode Island was the only state still restricting the vote to landowners, and the allotment of representatives to the various towns under the 1663 charter bore no relationship to their current population. Thomas Wilson Dorr, a prominent legislator, and his followers drafted a more equitable "People's Constitution" for the state, succeeded in getting it ratified by popular vote, and duly elected a slate of officials that included Dorr as governor. When the incumbents refused to recognize the new regime and tried to have Dorr arrested, an armed uprising ensued, led by Dorr himself. State troops were called out, and once again the college had to shut down while its buildings were used as barracks. The rebellion failed (with no loss of life on either side), but it made its point: By 1843, the state had a new constitution that extended suffrage and redressed some of the imbalances in representation.

After college life returned to normal, no action was taken on Wayland's 1841 report, probably because there seemed to be no pressing reason to do so. The institution appeared to be in good health – so it struck the university like a thunderclap when Wayland abruptly resigned in 1849, the day after Commencement. A gradual but steady decline in enrollment over the previous decade had led him to conclude that something was fundamentally wrong, and that drastic action was needed to correct Brown's course. The decrease in enrollment also meant, of course, increasing financial pressures – and after Nicholas Brown's death in 1841 there was no comparable source of much-needed funds.

Wayland's resignation was meant to shock the Corporation into acting, and it did. Members begged him to resume office and appointed him head of a Committee of Advice to reshape Brown's future. The committee's report, delivered in March 1850, quickly became famous nationwide as one of the most radical proposals yet made for restructuring an American college. Actually, as Bronson points out, the ideas were a continuation of Wayland's earlier writings, and some had long been in use at the University of Virginia. Nonetheless, the report excited a lot of comment, most of it positive, and it was implemented at Brown with little opposition.

The report was essentially a marketing plan that began by acknowledging that "with the present century, a new era dawned upon the world. A host of new sciences arose, all holding important relations to the progress of civilization." College curricula

Theatrics at Brown got their start after the Civil War, when the short-lived Thalian Dramatic Association gave way to the more durable Hammer & Tongs in 1867. Under the direction of Tom Crosby, H&T staged a yearly student-written "entertainment" at the Providence Opera House, because Brown had no stage of its own.

The Women's College organized its own dramatic society, Komians, in 1901; its male counterpart, Sock & Buskin, staged its first production a year later. For nearly 30 years, both societies carried on impersonating each other's gender – the women laboring under the extra handicap of being forbidden to wear male costumes. Sock & Buskin began using female actors in 1931 (the same year Faunce House Theater was built), and the two groups merged a decade later. Ben Brown, class of 1919, Sock & Buskin's director from 1921 to 1955, brought Brown theater to a new level of professionalism – presenting a

Above, a scene from Facing the Music, *a melodrama staged by Sock and Buskin in 1910. One of Rites and Reason's stellar performers was Sandra Franklin '75, shown below as Hannah in* Letters from a New England Negro.

full theater season, tackling playwrights from the ancient Greeks to G.B. Shaw, taking shows on the road.

Other established theater groups are Brownbrokers, founded in 1935 to stage original musicals; Production Workshop, for student-written and -produced works; and Rites & Reason, the research and development theater for Afro-American Studies.

had necessarily expanded, but the four years allotted for a bachelor's degree hadn't altered – and the result, the report argued, was a hasty and superficial review of many fields that left students ill prepared to practice in any of them. "Where are our classical scholars?...where are our mathematicians?" the report asked. It alluded to the pressures created by industrialization and westward expansion: "There has existed for the last twenty years a great demand for civil engineers....We presume the single academy at West Point...has done more towards the construction of railroads than all our one hundred and twenty colleges united."

The problems of superficiality and declining enrollments were both to be met by "adapt[ing] the article produced, to the wants of the community." This meant fewer required courses and more electives, so that students might pursue their chosen field in depth; making the length of the program more flexible, including a new three-year Ph.B. degree; and the addition of courses in agriculture, law, civil engineering, and chemistry and science applied to the arts. This last was especially tailored to Rhode Island, with its burgeoning textile, jewelry, and metal industries.

The "New System," despite its attempt to be both high-minded and practical, was an ironic reversal of Wayland's early efforts to raise academic standards at Brown. Admission requirements were eased to attract more students; the list of requirements for an A.B. degree was reduced by one-fourth, and an A.M. degree could now be earned for the same amount of work once entailed in getting an A.B. The inescapable result was that, although enrollments did increase for a few years, the value of a Brown degree was debased, and the quality of the students it attracted suffered. Both students and faculty were acutely conscious of this loss of prestige.

Albert Harkness (class of 1842) was professor of classics at Brown (1855–92) and a founder of the American School of Classical Studies in Athens. His son, Albert Granger Harkness, joined the Brown faculty in 1889 as associate professor of Latin and later served as director of the American School of Classical Studies in Rome.

It is difficult to imagine that Wayland himself could have been oblivious to the disappointing results of his New System. The fatigue which he pleaded as his reason for stepping down in 1855 may have been partly due to a sense of failure. But it didn't prevent him from staying involved with the University in a variety of official and unofficial capacities, including serving as a Fellow on the Corporation from 1855 to 1858. He was still a commanding figure, both in the University and in the larger community, when he died of a stroke in September 1865.

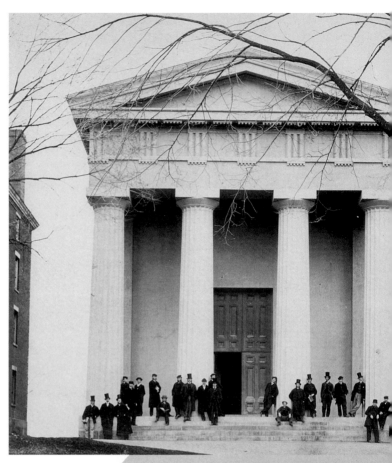

Manning Hall, a product of the Classical Revival, was built in 1835 by Nicholas Brown to house the college's library and chapel.

Tree planting efforts were underway in the 1860s, when the campus extended east from Rogers Hall (now the Salomon Center for Teaching) to Hope Street.

4 | *Building a University*

The man who succeeded Francis Wayland faced a double challenge: to rebuild Brown's academic reputation, weakened by the New System, and to do so without giving offense. Wayland himself was now a Fellow of the University, and most members of the Corporation had supported his academic reforms. But Barnas Sears, class of 1825, who took office in 1855, had both the authority and the tact to meet that challenge. He was a former president of Newton Theological Institution who had succeeded the renowned Horace Mann, class of 1819, as head of the Massachusetts Board of Education. He brought with him to Brown the highest reputation as a teacher and scholar, and a gift for diplomacy that (in contrast to Wayland's autocratic manner) smoothed many rough roads.

Sears's unpublished report to the Executive Board in 1856 "frankly and fearlessly probe[d] the wound," in Walter Bronson's words, yet was careful not to attack the quality of teaching or the courses themselves – only the lowered degree requirements. The report called them "an open act of underbidding other colleges," which had resulted in the best students choosing to go elsewhere, and in Brown being "flooded by a class of young men of little solidity or earnestness of character, who resort to this college...for the sake of cheap honors." There was no arguing with the facts Sears presented, and the Corporation in 1857 voted to restore the requirements and admission standards for the A.B. and A.M. degrees to essentially what they had been before the New System. Interestingly, the students themselves, despite their supposed intellectual laziness, welcomed these changes and objected strongly to the continuation

The First Rhode Island Regiment left downtown Providence on April 20, 1861, and later fought under General Ambrose Burnside at Bull Run, where Sullivan Ballou '52 (inset) was fatally wounded.

of the three-year Ph.B. program. (It finally became a four-year degree in 1876.)

Sears further endeared himself to students by relaxing the iron grip of college regulations a bit. Clubs and organizations were allowed to meet in the evenings, and the popular tradition of lighting candles in the windows of University Hall and Hope College on Commencement eve was restored. The two sports that dominated the campus in the nineteenth century, baseball and crew, had their beginnings in this era. Some beginnings were more auspicious than others: The student baseball club defeated Providence's best town club in 1864, but Brown's first entry in an intercollegiate boat race in 1859 was a six-oared shell, *Atalanta*, that weighed 150 pounds more than her rivals from Harvard and Yale, and was not even in sight of the finish line when those two crossed it. The following year the Brown crew tried to remedy the error by entering the 112-pound *Brunonia* – which was so fragile it broke up and sank halfway through the race. Mercifully, the hiatus caused by the Civil War gave the Brown crew a chance to get itself organized.

The hiatus was only an extracurricular one; classes and Commencements went on more or less as usual, and enrollment remained fairly stable through the war, although the University, like the rest of the country, was galvanized by these momentous

B. WILLIAMS

events. From the start there was no shortage of Brown volunteers: 268 students and alumni served in the war, 132 of them from the five classes that graduated between 1861 and 1865. The first Brown man to die was Maj. Sullivan Ballou '52, made famous by the PBS series "The Civil War" for the deeply moving letter he wrote to his wife shortly before he was fatally wounded at Bull Run. By the war's end, Brown had lost twenty more.

The war also deprived Sears, one of Brown's ablest presidents, of the opportunity to leave a more lasting mark. Still, the achievements of his twelve-year tenure were considerable. Not only was the University's academic reputation salvaged, but endowment increased by $120,000, scholarships by $36,000, faculty salaries were raised, and a much-needed chemical laboratory was built. Sears's excellent relationships with his various constituencies – faculty, students, community leaders – did much to restore confidence in Brown and laid the foundation for its phenomenal growth in the late nineteenth century.

When Sears retired in 1867, the Corporation's first two choices to succeed him – Martin Anderson, president of the University of Rochester, and Ezekiel Robinson, president of Rochester Theological Seminary – both declined the invitation. Brown then turned to one of its own. Alexis Caswell '22 had served thirty-six years as professor of mathematics and natural philosophy, retiring in 1864, and had been acting president in 1840–41 (during Wayland's trip to Europe) and regent in 1852–55. He stepped into the breach once again and succeeded in being more than just a caretaker president. Between 1868 and 1872, the nearly defunct alumni association was revived and greatly enlarged, the

An elegant Slater Hall room shows the Victorian tastes of an earlier generation of students.

CHARLES EVANS HUGHES
CLASS OF 1881

Charles Evans Hughes, class of 1881, grew his famous beard in 1890 in the interest of efficiency – to save trips to the barber. At the time he had a busy commercial law practice in New York, with a side interest in Republican reform politics. In 1905 his reformist career began in earnest as counsel to state legislative committees investigating abuses in the New York City utilities industry and the insurance business. The resulting renown enabled him to run against and beat William Randolph Hearst for governor of New York in 1906. After his second term, President William Howard Taft named him to the Supreme Court, but Hughes hadn't quite gotten elective politics out of his system. He resigned from the court to challenge Woodrow Wilson for the presidency in 1916, and lost. He returned to corporate law, then was recalled to public life from 1921–25 as secretary of state under Warren Harding and Calvin Coolidge. By 1930, when Herbert Hoover named him Chief Justice of the Supreme Court, Hughes was the "acknowledged leader of the American bar." With magisterial authority and aplomb, he steered the court through one of the most turbulent periods in American history – respecting legal precedent while responding to the harsh new realities of the Depression, taking strong stands in favor of civil liberties and civil rights, even outmaneuvering FDR's attempt to "pack" the court. Most importantly, in helping define the government's role in managing the economy, Hughes became "one of the master builders of the American federal system."

MARY EMMA WOOLLEY
CLASS OF 1894

On December 31, 1900, Mary Emma Woolley, class of 1894, the new president of Mount Holyoke College, arrived on the campus in South Hadley, Mass., ready to assume her duties on New Year's Day of a new century. Waiting for her was a basket of fresh eggs from the chairman of the botany department with a card reading, "Nineteenth Century eggs for a Twentieth Century President." Woolley had already established herself as a pioneer by being one of the first two women to graduate from Brown; she went on to accumulate a long list of such firsts in her lifetime. She was the first woman to serve as chair of the College Entrance Examination Board, the first woman elected to the Senate of Phi Beta Kappa, the first to represent the United States at a major international conference (the 1932 Disarmament Conference in Geneva). She felt strongly that women must "do their share of the world's thinking and working," and she was appalled when, after thirty-seven years of promoting female leadership and scholarship as president of Mount Holyoke, the trustees chose a man as her successor. Her bitterness in retirement was eased somewhat when Brown awarded her the Rosenberger Medal in 1937. She already had an honorary doctorate from Brown (one of 20 honorary degrees from institutions around the country), and she was the first woman to receive both honors from her alma mater.

Mary Woolley and Anne Tillinghast Weeden entered Brown with advanced standing in 1891 and became its first women graduates in 1894.

Advisory and Executive Committee of the Corporation was created, endowment nearly doubled, and two more endowed chairs, both in the sciences, were established: the Hazard chair in physics and the Rogers chair in chemistry. In July 1870, the freshman crew vindicated Brown's prewar record by beating Harvard, Yale, and Amherst in the annual regatta on Lake Quinsigamond in Worcester, Mass.

The new endowed chairs in physics and chemistry highlighted the profound changes taking place in college curricula – the decline of theology and oratory ("that source of power and influence in this Republic," as one commentator put it during Wayland's era) and the rise of the applied sciences. Far from being merely a change in emphasis, it marked the shift from a rhetorical to an empirical mind-set. "The scientific spirit was permeating every department of thought," Bronson observes, "and arousing multitudes to a new realization of the value of trained intellect in confronting the problems of life on all its levels." Ironically, the man who was to carry forward the banner of scientific inquiry at Brown was a professor of divinity and seminary president who had already turned down the presidency of Brown once: Ezekiel Gilman Robinson, class of 1838.

Robinson, still the head of Rochester Theological Seminary, did not refuse the Corporation when it again approached him in 1872 after Caswell's retirement. He resolved to "strike at once for a widened curriculum and new buildings," and years later he described in his autobiography the impact of his academic policy: "Naturally there was a jostling of old hereditary prejudices in behalf of certain studies which from time immemorial had taken precedence of all others. But science then got a foothold in the curriculum which it is never likely to lose." So did subjects like modern languages and English literature, which also found their way into admission requirements. Robinson's first annual report to the Corporation showed the range of his ambitions: ". . . A large number of the intelligent citizens of our state are now desirous that a SCIENTIFIC SCHOOL of high order – [with] sub-schools of Design, of Drawing, of Civil Engineering, of Architecture, of the Fine Arts, etc. – may speedily be established in Rhode Island, and if possible may be established in conjunction with, and in a sense, as a part of Brown University."

Robinson, of course, was essentially describing the Rhode Island School of Design, founded four years after that report.

Engineering remained part of Brown's curriculum, and architecture had its day too, but Brown could not afford to become an art school as well. It had other priorities, such as classroom and laboratory space, dorm space, a larger library, and repairing University Hall, which had become "an eyesore and a reproach," in the president's words. Sayles Hall, Slater Hall, and Wilson Hall all date from the Robinson era, and John Carter Brown's death in 1874 brought a bequest of land and money to build a new library (now Robinson Hall). The fate of University Hall, battered by generations of service as a dormitory, hung in the balance for a while. One contingent actually proposed demolishing it – but luckily, the *grande dame* of the campus was proven to be structurally sound, and $50,000 was raised to renovate it.

Ezekiel G. Robinson '38, Brown's seventh president (1872–89).

The broadening of the curriculum under Robinson made it possible finally for Brown to become a true university, with a full range of degree programs. In 1886, toward the end of his tenure, Robinson stated in his annual report, "The time, it seems to me, has now fully come for Brown University to offer a course of

A chemistry class of the 1870s posed with its equipment on the steps of Rogers Hall.

study to be pursued by candidates for the degree of Doctor of Philosophy." The following year the Corporation authorized the establishment of a Ph.D. program, and in 1889 the first doctoral degrees were awarded. When Robinson retired in March of that year, the stage had been set for one of the greatest periods of expansion in Brown's history.

Rhode Island and the nation were then at the pinnacle of the Gilded Age, an era of enormous affluence in which the middle class shared as well as the wealthy. Rhode Island, as William McLoughlin notes, had acquired a clout far beyond its size: Sen. Nelson W. Aldrich, who controlled the tariff schedules in Congress, was known as the "General Manager of the United States"; the "Four Hundred" summered in Newport every year and built the mansions for which the city is still famous; and the manufacturers who dominated the state's economy traveled in the same circles as the nation's richest and most powerful people.

❦ JOHN D. ROCKEFELLER JR.
CLASS OF 1897

John D. Rockefeller Jr. refused honorary degrees from all institutions, but accepted an L.L.D. from Brown in 1937. In 1950, he donated $6 million to the University.

In 1893, the only son of the world's wealthiest man chose Brown as his college because he knew he would feel "lost in the crowd" at Yale. Intensely shy and private, John D. Rockefeller Jr., class of 1897, found a camaraderie at Brown that helped him come at least partly out of his shell (he was elected president of the junior class and senior manager of the football team), and he treasured those memories all his life. It also helped prepare him for the relentlessly public life he led as the steward of an immense fortune. "Johnny Rock's" relationship with his powerful father was one of mutual affection and admiration, but he chose a very different path: that of philanthropy. He believed sincerely that wealth should be "an instrumentality of constructive social living," and he used it wherever he thought it could make a real difference. From massive public health campaigns to eradicate hookworm and other diseases, to the restoration of Colonial Williamsburg and the dedication of new national parks, to providing a home site for the United Nations and funneling millions of dollars into colleges and universities, the Rockefeller Foundation he established set the standard for "big giving" and left almost no aspect of American life untouched.

But the immigrants (then mostly Irish and French Canadian) who staffed the factories and made possible the state's wealth were also a growing threat to the hegemony of Yankee Protestants. The latter resorted to a variety of strategies to maintain control, from political corruption to social one-upmanship. As Theodore Crane explains it, in the late nineteenth century, college education "at last [began] to appeal widely to middle-class families, particularly...among those of old-stock ancestry troubled by the influx of non-Protestant immigrants."

Onto this fertile ground stepped Elisha Benjamin Andrews '70, a professor at Cornell, former Brown faculty member, and former president of Denison University in Ohio. Andrews, a combat veteran who had lost an eye in the siege of Petersburg, was by all accounts a charismatic and vivid personality; during his five years on the Brown faculty, he had become the object of hero worship by students, and was the overwhelmingly popular choice to succeed President Robinson in 1889. "At his touch," Bronson writes, "the old college leaped into new life, and began to grow at an astonishing rate" – much faster than other New England colleges in this period. Enrollment "began to rise like the incoming tide": from 276 undergraduates to 641 in the first eight years, and from three graduate students to 117 in only six years. Professorships increased from sixteen to thirty-seven as Andrews recruited trained specialists from all over the country, and academic departments grew from seventeen to twenty-five.

Andrews also served as the catalyst for another landmark in Brown's evolution: the admission of women. The subject had been broached several times in the past two decades (one woman had actually applied for admission in 1874 and been refused), but the Corporation had repeatedly stalled it. It was the Quaker members of that body who began to lobby for coeducation in the 1880s. One of them, the poet John Greenleaf Whittier,

Pembroke Hall was under construction in 1897 when the Class of 1900 gathered for this portrait.

wrote to a friend that it was a matter of "simple justice." President Robinson had studied the issue, and in 1886 had recommended the creation of "a distinct but appended college" for women. The Corporation approved the plan, but again postponed action, until President Andrews took over and got the ball rolling. In 1891 women were finally admitted as candidates for all University degrees.

Women undergraduates, however, were not admitted to University classrooms. Instruction was provided by a few professors who volunteered their services (to be paid for by students' fees), and classes were held in the University Grammar School, in Andrews's office, and in other buildings in the neighborhood as space permitted. The course content was identical with that of the men's courses, though, and Bronson notes that "the average standing of the women students was regularly higher than that of the men in corresponding classes." The physics professor in 1895–96 wrote that he wished "to bear testimony to the uniformly admirable work done by the women. I began the course of lectures to the Women's College with diffidence, believing that the mind of woman is not, as a rule, of a kind to be willingly tethered by exact considerations of the material universe. But I found neither lack of aptitude nor of grasp."

The first two women, Anne Weeden and Mary Woolley, graduated in 1894; by 1896–97 there were 157 female undergraduates, thirty-one graduate students, and a college building nearing completion. Pembroke Hall, named after Roger Williams's college at Cambridge University, was dedicated in 1897. But the growth of the Women's College was overshadowed at the time by a crisis in the academic community. On the surface, it was about the arcane issue of "free silver" (i.e., unrestricted coinage

VOLUME XXX.

NEW YORK, AUGUST 26, 1897.

NUMBER 766.

Entered at the New York Post Office as Second-Class Mail Matter.
Copyright, 1897, by MITCHELL & MILLER.

HOW TO BUILD UP A UNIVERSITY.

of silver), which had dominated the 1896 presidential race – and about the not-so-arcane issue of free speech. President Andrews had voiced his support of free silver, a view that was out of favor with many on the Corporation, and they in turn tried to muzzle him. In a written statement delivered to him in July 1897, they asserted that his views "were so contrary to the views generally held by the friends of the University that the University had already lost gifts and legacies," and they asked him to keep silent on the subject. Andrews promptly resigned, stating that he refused to surrender "that reasonable liberty of utterance...in the absence of which the most ample endowment for an educational institution would have but little worth." A national furor erupted over the issue of academic freedom, and prominent academics from all over the country, as well as Brown faculty and alumni, rallied around Andrews. The besieged Corporation backed down, and Andrews withdrew his resignation.

The underlying issue, though, as the Corporation's written statement showed, was financial – and that had not been resolved. Andrews had launched an ambitious fund drive at the beginning of the decade, aiming to raise $1 million within a year and another $2 million within ten years. But the Panic of 1893 intervened and the campaign fell flat. As enrollment continued to grow, resources were strained beyond capacity. The only additions to the Brown campus after 1891 were Maxcy Hall, Ladd Observatory, and Lyman Gym, and the University was often operating in the red. It was easy to pin the blame on Andrews for overreaching, for lack of prudence or failure to cultivate donors properly. In fact, what the Corporation did (as Theodore Crane has pointed out) was repudiate bold presidential leadership. The strain in their relationship with Andrews was irreversible, and he resigned for good in 1898.

The Corporation's attempt to stifle President Andrews's political views only made it a target of ridicule, as this Life *magazine cover shows.*

The Class of 1906, at right, won the intramural basketball championship their senior year.

The 1999–2000 women's ice hockey team, left, celebrates its ECAC championship.

From the time the Women's College established a Department of Physical Culture in 1897 until after World War II, the motto of female athletics at Brown was, in the words of physical education director (1930–1961) Bessie Rudd, "Let the women have their sports and the men have theirs." Most women's sports were intramural, offered as part of the physical education program. Among the most popular were swimming, basketball, tennis, field hockey, lacrosse, and bowling.

By the mid-1960s, however, the genteel "ladies" model was fading at Brown, and modern programs began to emerge under the leadership of Director of Physical Education Arlene Gorton '52. In 1964, Gorton helped Pembroke students establish the first women's college ice hockey team in the nation; today their legacy lives on in Brown's ECAC champion women's hockey team and its two gold-medal Olympians, Katie King '97 and Tara Mounsey '01.

As Pembroke and Brown merged in the early 1970s, Title IX, the federal statute prohibiting sex discrimination in higher education, put male and female sports on a more equal footing. In the ensuing years Brown added varsity women's programs faster than did most other universities. Today Brown has 37 varsity sports – 20 for women and 17 for men – comprising one of the largest NCAA Division I programs in the country. Even so, in 1992, when the University attempted to trim its budget by cutting two women's teams (volleyball and gymnastics), along with men's wrestling and golf, Brown became the target of a class-action Title IX lawsuit brought by one of the gymnasts. Eventually Brown settled the case and took further measures to equalize the numbers of men and women in its varsity programs.

Today, women's teams are among the University's most successful. Recent years have seen Brown women win the national championship in women's crew; ECAC championships in field hockey and ice hockey; Ivy championships in volleyball, softball, and tennis; and the women's cross-country Heptagonal championship.

Andrews's legacy of high academic standards and a wider reputation for Brown was a permanent one. His successor, William H.P. Faunce '80, who was academically little more than a "cautious caretaker" of the University for the next thirty years, presided over the unfinished part of Andrews's vision: an unprecedented era of physical expansion. The John Carter Brown Library, John Hay Library, Faunce House (née Rockefeller Hall), Sayles Gym, Miller Hall, Caswell Hall, and the Van Wickle Gates all date from the first three decades of the twentieth century, when Brown finally began to catch up with itself.

Augustus Stout Van Wickle, class of 1876 (inset), left a bequest to build Brown's celebrated Van Wickle Gates, dedicated in 1901. The gates are opened only twice each year – inward to admit students at the start of the academic year and outward at Commencement to discharge them. A plaque with a quotation from Cicero was added in 1906: "These studies fortify one's youth, delight one's old age: amid success they are an ornament, in failure they are a refuge and a comfort."

Architect's rendering of the "Men's Dormitory Group" (Wriston Quadrangle) in 1950.

Within a year the site had been cleared for construction. This project gave a boost to President Wriston's vision of Brown becoming a national university, as it provided a substantial increase in residential housing on campus.

5 | *The Modern Era*

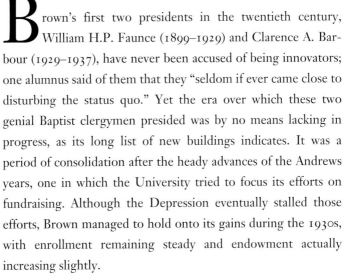

Brown's first two presidents in the twentieth century, William H.P. Faunce (1899–1929) and Clarence A. Barbour (1929–1937), have never been accused of being innovators; one alumnus said of them that they "seldom if ever came close to disturbing the status quo." Yet the era over which these two genial Baptist clergymen presided was by no means lacking in progress, as its long list of new buildings indicates. It was a period of consolidation after the heady advances of the Andrews years, one in which the University tried to focus its efforts on fundraising. Although the Depression eventually stalled those efforts, Brown managed to hold onto its gains during the 1930s, with enrollment remaining steady and endowment actually increasing slightly.

This was also the era of Brown's first brush with football greatness (the Rose Bowl team of 1915 and Tuss McLaughry's "Iron Men" of 1926); the heyday of college humor magazines like the *Brown Jug*, where S. J. Perelman '25 cut his teeth; the maturation of the Women's College, officially renamed Pembroke in 1928; and the revision of Brown's original charter in 1926 to eliminate the requirement of a Baptist president. Faunce, himself a man of the cloth, was the prime mover behind this change. When he retired in 1929, the Corporation's new freedom of choice gave its members a distinguished candidate in Zechariah Chafee '07, professor of law at Harvard and a nationally known civil libertarian. The Baptists were not quite ready to give up the helm, however, and they prevailed in their choice of Clarence Barbour, class of 1888, president (like Robinson before him) of Rochester Theological Seminary.

Barbour kept Brown on a steady course during the worst

Frederick D. "Fritz" Pollard '19, considered one of the finest running backs in the history of college football, was a star of Brown's 1916 Rose Bowl team. (Brown lost, 14-0.)

The "Iron Men" of 1926, Brown's only undefeated football team, who earned their reputation in the Yale Bowl against a heavily favored Eli team.

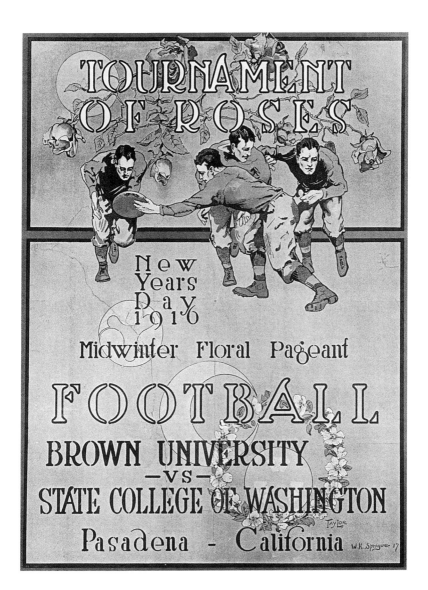

TOURNAMENT OF ROSES

New Years Day 1916

Midwinter Floral Pageant

FOOTBALL

BROWN UNIVERSITY
—vs—
STATE COLLEGE OF WASHINGTON

Pasadena - California

W.K. Sprague '17

years of the Depression, but he did not outlive it; illness forced him to take a leave of absence in 1936, and he died in January 1937. His death marked the end of 173 years of sectarian leadership of an increasingly secular university. The pace of change on all fronts – social, political, technological – was accelerating rapidly, and the times demanded that universities be progressive and flexible enough to keep up. Even the conservative Corporation recognized this, in choosing as Brown's next president a man who was not at all afraid to challenge the status quo. Henry Merritt Wriston was neither a Baptist nor a Brown alumnus nor a product of the "Eastern establishment." Born in the Wyoming Territory in 1889, he went on to earn a Ph.D. in history from Harvard and a reputation as an innovator as president of Lawrence College in Wisconsin. William S. Learned '97 of the Carnegie Corporation, in recommending Wriston to a friend on the Brown Corporation, wrote, "He would undoubtedly provide a series of shocks to the old college, but I believe it would survive and profit enormously."

Henry Merritt Wriston, Brown's eleventh president (1937–55), was regarded as one of the finest college presidents of his era.

He was right on all counts. Wriston in 1937 took over an essentially regional institution and, in the course of the next eighteen years, transformed it into a major American university. No aspect of University life was left untouched, which meant that Wriston had to do battle from time to time with a variety of vested interests: the Corpo-

Margaret Shove Morriss, affectionately known as "Peggy Push" during her twenty-seven years as dean of Pembroke (1923–1950), did indeed propel the college to national standing – attracting students from around the country and abroad, doubling enrollment to 800, expanding its physical facilities, and changing its name from simply the Women's College to Pembroke. A Baltimore-born Quaker with strong Quaker convictions about justice and equity, Morriss was outspoken on the subject of opportunities for women, saying, "I don't think society is just in giving all this training to women if it is not going to be used." She came to Providence from Mount Holyoke, where she was associate professor of history during the presidency of Mary Woolley '94, and she became a full professor of history at Pembroke in addition to the deanship. She served as president of the American Association of University Women and the New England Associa-

tion of Colleges and Secondary Schools, as a member of the Committee on Higher Education of the American Council on Education, and as a consultant to the secretary of war during World War II. In 1965 the AAUW established an international fellowship in her name to support postgraduate and doctoral studies by women.

Button-cute, rapier-keen, cucumber-cool, and gall-bitter." That pithy description could only fit one man: S. J. Perelman, class of 1925. Perelman grew up in Providence wanting to be a cartoonist. He got his start on the *Brown Jug* as an undergraduate, which led to a job with the weekly magazine *Judge* after he left Brown in 1924. He found his captions getting longer and longer, until he was no longer a cartoonist but a writer. Within a decade he was writing screenplays for the Marx Brothers (*Monkey Business* and *Horse Feathers*), followed by stage plays and musicals (*One Touch of Venus*, *The Beauty Part*), countless humor pieces for the *New Yorker*, and the Oscar-winning screenplay for *Around the World in 80 Days*. Perelman's prose was dense as a fruit-cake with puns, wordplays, and allusions:

"The following morning the *Maid of Hull*, a frigate of the line mounting 36 guns, out of Bath and into bed in a twinkling, dropped downstairs on the tide, bound for Bombay, object matrimony...." He died in 1979 before he had a chance to write his autobiography, tentatively titled *The Hindsight Saga*.

Andrews Hall of Pembroke College, shown here in the early 1950s, was dedicated in 1947 and named in honor of President Elisha Benjamin Andrews, who helped secure the admission of women to Brown.

ration, the faculty, fraternities, alumni, East Side neighbors, and so on. (William Learned had warned him, "The old mores weigh appallingly at some points, and you will doubtless feel on more than one occasion like using dynamite.") He brought to these battles a combination of intellectual keenness, political shrewdness, and moral conviction – but he seems to have prevailed, as often as not, by the sheer force of his personality.

Wriston's first challenge, as a non-Baptist and non-alumnus, was to "become legitimate," particularly in the eyes of the Corporation. He did so by showing himself to be a man of both vision and decisive action. One of his first acts as president, intended to "awaken a decent pride" in Brown, was to order the director of admissions to admit no one who had been turned down elsewhere. Later he made it even more stringent, requiring that successful applicants list Brown as their first choice on the College Entrance Examination form. The result was that Brown acquired a reputation for being hard to get into, and both the number and quality of applicants increased. (Being an "Ivy League" school didn't mean as much in those days; the Ivy Group, which had existed as an informal football association since 1900, wasn't officially organized until 1954, and then only to set policies for intercollegiate athletic competition.)

Wriston's next priority was to rebuild Brown's sense of community by making it a residential college once again. Housing had not kept pace with enrollment over the years, and Wriston was determined to gather his flock back onto campus. The answer to the housing shortage was Wriston Quad, and at Pembroke, Andrews Hall. To make way for the quad, a number of historic houses had to be demolished; when the president described this as "the greatest slum clearance since Sherman burned Atlanta," Brown's neighbors woke up and organized the Providence Preservation Society. The quad was also meant to be the answer to the problem of Brown's fraternities, which till then had been in chapter-owned houses on the fringes of campus. Many were financially strapped, and the condition of their chapter houses showed it. Wriston made them all turn over their houses to the University, in exchange for new quarters in the quad and private dining rooms in the refectory – a move intended to strengthen both the Brown community and the fraternities themselves, although some of them were less than grateful at first.

Another priority was the curriculum. Wriston believed that education should not be limited to classroom learning ("an instructor up front and students in rows before him"), and over the objections of the faculty he reduced the number of required courses per semester from five to four. During World War II he appointed a committee to study the content of the curriculum, and its recommendations became the second so-called New Curriculum in Brown's history. Its core was a broad range of distri-

Rosemary Pierrel (Sorrentino) was Pembroke's sixth and last dean, serving from 1961 to 1971. An experimental psychologist and former faculty member at Barnard, she returned to teaching and research at Brown after the merger.

John Rowe Workman, one of Brown's most beloved professors, came from Princeton to teach classics in 1947. Before he retired in 1985, he had become a legend for his humor, his scholarship, and his direction of the Latin Carol Service each holiday season.

bution courses in the first two years, and it remained substantially unchanged until 1969. After the war Wriston introduced IC courses – Identification and Criticism of Ideas – which were seminar-like discussion groups for freshmen and sophomores. These were judged to be an interesting experiment, but not a very efficient use of faculty time, although they were reincarnated years later as Modes of Thought courses. Finally, Wriston saw to it that Brown and Pembroke had one and the same curriculum by eliminating separate classes and faculty for Pembrokers.

Another group Wriston successfully integrated into campus life was the returning veterans of World War II. Under his leadership, Brown was the only institution in Rhode Island to establish a Veterans College, and Wriston made it clear to the GIs who flooded the campus that they were not "stepchildren," but were entitled to all the rights and privileges of a Brown education. They proved to be a highly motivated group, and many went on to distinguish themselves academically.

In his quest to make Brown a first-rank university, Wriston was determined that its faculty should be second to none, and he exercised personal control over the selection and appointment process. A number of academic departments were developing national reputations, such as Applied Mathematics, which recruited several brilliant European scholars during the Second World War and made significant research contributions to the war effort. Two departments created during Wriston's tenure are unique to Brown: Egyptology and History of Mathematics. Wriston strongly supported research and scholarship, and refused to allow graduate study to be phased out as a cost-cutting measure, but he also blocked the creation of a separate graduate faculty. He believed in the concept of a university college (a phrase that had been used to describe Brown since the early 1900s), in which undergraduate teaching was the heart of the enterprise.

For over thirty years, Brown's History of Mathematics department, the only one in the world, was virtually synonymous with Otto Neugebauer, its founding chairman and professor. Neugebauer, an Austrian native, had studied mathematics and physics before becoming fascinated by Egyptology at the University of Göttingen. After writing his doctoral thesis on Egyptian fractions, he tackled Babylonian cuneiform tablets – specifically the highly sophisticated astronomical and mathematical texts, which had been deciphered but not really understood by previous scholars. Neugebauer's work revolutionized our modern understanding of the roots of science in antiquity; he discovered, for example, that the algebra and geometry used by the Greeks had been known to the Babylonians as much as 2,000 years earlier. He left Nazi-occupied Europe in 1939 to come to Brown, and in 1947 was made head of the new History of Mathematics department. The author of such landmark works as *The Exact Sciences in Antiquity* and *A History of Ancient Mathematical Astronomy*, Neugebauer received many of academia's most prestigious awards and honors, including election to the American Philosophical Society and the National Academy of Sciences. In 1960 he was named Florence Pirce Grant University Professor at Brown, and in 1987 he was awarded the Rosenberger Medal by the Brown faculty.

Brown today is still recognizably the institution Wriston shaped, and few would dispute that he was its greatest president. His distinction as an educator and historian led to an increasing involvement in national affairs before and after he stepped down in 1955. As a friend and adviser to Dwight Eisenhower, he was asked in 1954 to help reorganize the Foreign Service, and took a six-month leave from Brown to do so. Upon Wriston's retirement, Eisenhower made him director of the American Assembly, an organization that arranged conferences on current national problems, and in 1960 appointed him head of a blue-ribbon commission charged with identifying "the great issues of our generation." He also served as president of the Council on Foreign Relations, and continued writing and speaking on national issues until his death in 1978.

Brown's next president, Barnaby C. Keeney, was somewhat more of an insider than his famous predecessor: He had joined the faculty in 1946 as assistant professor of medieval history, then became dean of the Graduate School in 1949 and dean of the College in 1953. But Keeney, a much-decorated combat veteran, was no less blunt and outspoken, and every bit as ambitious for Brown. Embarking on a building campaign of heroic proportions, Keeney joked that Brown's neighbors would have to learn anew the meaning of "higher education," since lack of ground space would force many new buildings skyward. During his eleven-year tenure, the Rockefeller Library (dedicated in 1964 in honor of Brown's bicentennial celebration), Barus-Holley, J. Walter Wilson Lab, Hunter Lab, the Computer Lab

President Barnaby Keeney got the equivalent of a standing ovation at his last Commencement exercises in 1966.

(housing the first IBM 7070 owned by an Eastern university), Meehan Auditorium, and the West Quad (now Keeney Quad) were built. And Brown did acquire some significant chunks of ground space: the thirty-nine-acre grounds of Dexter Asylum, which became Aldrich-Dexter Field (site of the Erickson Athletic Complex), and the 376-acre Haffenreffer estate in Bristol.

The success of the building campaign was a testament to Keeney's skills as a fund raiser (Wriston said that his "gift for charming money from flint-like men of substance...is awe-inspiring") and to Brown's stature, which made it easier to attract large gifts. Citing its potential to "become one of the most important university centers in the country," the Ford Foundation twice honored Brown with major grants during the Keeney years, the first for $7.5 million and the second for $5 million – and both times Brown succeeded in raising the two-for-one matching funds. Not all the money went into buildings, of course. As befitted a former dean of the Graduate School, Keeney was strongly committed to graduate education, and graduate enrollment nearly tripled during his tenure. Plans for a medical school began to be discussed, and a six-year program leading to a Master of Medical Science degree was established in 1963.

By stepping down in 1966, Keeney managed to escape the scars inflicted on most university presidents – including his successors – by the student activism of the late '60s and early '70s. He went on to head the newly established National Endowment for the Humanities, while Brown's new president, Ray L. Heffner, was swept up in a social and political revolution that turned the campus on its ear. For perhaps the first time in the history of American universities, major changes were being impelled from the bottom up instead of from the top down. "Student power" was not just a catch phrase, but a startling new reality.

When Heffner, a reflective Elizabethan scholar who had been

Josiah S. Carberry, professor of psycho-ceramics (the study of cracked pots), has held tenure longer than anyone on the Brown faculty, past, present or future. He was born on a bulletin board in University Hall in 1929, in an anonymous notice: "On Thursday evening at 8:15 in Sayles Hall J. S. Carberry will give a lecture on 'Archaic Greek Architectural Revetments in Connection with Ionian Philosophy.' For tickets and further information apply to Professor John Spaeth." Professor Ben Clough, suspecting a

ruse, inserted the word "not" between "will" and "give." Spaeth had no tickets, but he rose to the occasion and provided further information: that Carberry had an ungrammatical wife, Laura; a poetical daughter Patricia; a puffin-hunting daughter Lois; and an accident-prone assistant named Truman Grayson, who was always being bitten by things beginning with "A."

The Carberry family proved to be prolific correspondents, sending letters, telegrams, and postcards, and inserting

notices about themselves in the local press until they were banned by the *Providence Journal*. But in other newspapers, in directories that published Carberry's name, and in journals that carried his articles, his friends kept his spirit alive. Likewise, they honored him by making every Friday the 13th Carberry Day – a custom begun on Friday, May 13, 1955, when the University received an anonymous gift of $101.01 to establish the Josiah S. Carberry Fund. Henceforth, every Carberry Day members of the Brown community have donated loose change to the fund to purchase "such books as Professor Carberry might or might not approve of." In gratitude for his continuing support, the University Library has named its on-line catalogue Josiah.

vice president and dean of faculty at Indiana University, came to Brown in 1966, there were already stirrings of unrest, primarily over the college's *in loco parentis* role. Students were objecting to curfews for women undergraduates (when men had none) and rules restricting visits by the opposite sex in dorm rooms. The ferment spread quickly to issues like the curriculum, the role of minorities at Brown, the increasingly unpopular Vietnam war, and the place of ROTC on campus. By 1968, things were coming to a head. Ira Magaziner '69 and Elliot Maxwell '68 released their famous report calling for sweeping curricular changes at Brown. Black students organized a walkout in December to protest the University's minority recruitment and admission policies. Objections to ROTC's presence on campus escalated into a confrontation with the Advisory and Executive Committee, when 150 students crashed the April 1969 meeting to demand that ROTC be ousted.

Ira Magaziner '69 and President Ray Heffner conferred often in 1968–69 as the debate over the proposed New Curriculum heated up.

Wbru-fm, which bills itself as "Southern New England's Only Modern Rock," has stayed ahead of the pack through most of its history. The first college radio station in the country, it was started in 1936 by two freshmen who linked their dorm rooms in Caswell and Littlefield halls by wire. Thirty years later it got an FM license, incorporated as Brown Broadcasting (an independent nonprofit entity), and launched itself into the "real world" of commercial radio.

wbru-fm brought album-oriented rock to the Providence market in the late sixties and seventies – the first rock station to break from a Top 40 format. Over the years, as its format has evolved, wbru-fm has continued to define its own niche. Currently it is the only station in the Providence market that focuses on modern rock. It is also the home of *360 Degree Black Experience in Sound*, an "urban contemporary" program that runs all day Sunday and covers everything from gospel to rap. From its homegrown beginnings in Hope College, 'bru has become big business, with a volunteer staff of some 150 students and interns and annual revenues in excess of $2.4 million for the 1999 fiscal year.

wbru's success and growing audience of listeners has not gone unnoticed nationally. In 1993, 1994, and 1995, *Rolling Stone* magazine named wbru radio station of the year in the medium market category – the only station in the

In May 1940, George Stuckert '42, at top, and Edward Sarnoff '42, son of RCA president David Sarnoff, strung transmission lines on a Slater Hall chimney for the first broadcast of the Intercollegiate Broadcasting System, composed of twelve northeastern colleges.

country to win this award three years in a row. In 1997, wbru's accolades included nominations from *Billboard/ Monitor Magazine* for best radio station, best program director, and best music director. wbru-fm was honored again by *Rolling Stone* in 1998 when it was selected as one of the top ten radio stations in the United States.

Although the upheavals at Brown were relatively restrained and never reached the level of violence and polarization seen on many campuses, they were more than Ray Heffner was prepared to handle. The month after the ROTC showdown, he wearily offered his resignation, stating, "I have simply reached the conclusion that I do not enjoy being a university president." That same May, after more than a year of vigorous debate, the faculty held a marathon meeting and voted final approval of the New Curriculum – the third in Brown's 200-year history, and by far the most radical.

In 1968, hundreds of students listened to marathon faculty debates on curricular reform via loudspeakers on the Green.

*A bird's-eye view of the campus
looking west from the fourteen-story
sciences library.*

6 | *The International University*

What made the New Curriculum truly radical (and unique) was its redefinition of the role and responsibilities of undergraduates. By eliminating distribution requirements and "core" courses outside the concentration, it gave students a large measure of control over their own education. In doing so, the New Curriculum recalled some of the principles of Wayland's curricular reforms a century earlier, particularly his belief that a student should be able to study "what he chose, all that he chose, and only what he chose." By making letter grades optional, it encouraged students to explore unfamiliar or difficult subjects. And it acknowledged (as Wayland had in his time) that the accelerating "information explosion" made it unrealistic to imagine that any college could imbue all students with the same basic, essential information – even if it were possible to agree on what that necessary core of knowledge was.

Instead of seeing higher education as primarily a fact-gathering process, with students expected to assimilate a certain quota of facts from various disciplines, the New Curriculum emphasized the importance of understanding *how* those disciplines tackled their subject matter and constructed reality. Modes of Thought courses, a cornerstone of the 1969 curriculum, were designed to explore various approaches to knowledge, encourage critical thinking that transcended disciplinary boundaries, and lay a foundation for independent studies. Again, the New Curriculum was not really so new or so radical a departure from Brown's past: In 1958–59, Professor George Morgan had introduced such a perspective in the first extradepartmental University Course, titled "Modes of Experience: Science, History, Philosophy, and the Arts."

Even though Morgan's course was far outside the academic mainstream at the time, it had President Keeney's blessing. Keeney, in fact, had told Morgan that he thought undergraduate education lacked vitality and coherence, and that the trend toward academic specialization was too strong. The course inspired other faculty to try integrative approaches (in courses with titles such as "Science and Civilization" and "The Functions of Litera-

ture"), and it attracted gifted undergraduates who were looking for a new kind of intellectual challenge. Among them were Elliot Maxwell and Ira Magaziner, who enrolled in Morgan's Modes of Experience course. Magaziner went on to concentrate in human studies – Brown's first interdisciplinary concentration, developed by Morgan in 1967.

This emphasis on integrating knowledge was to become a basic principle of the New Curriculum and a hallmark of Brown's evolution in the 1970s and 1980s. But before the cur-

The establishment of Brown's M.D.-granting medical school in 1975 was a turning point for regional health care.

riculum's potential could be realized and that evolution could flourish, the University had to overcome a number of obstacles. In the midst of the political and social turmoil of the era, Brown faced some painful internal struggles: absorbing Pembroke College in 1971; launching a full-fledged medical school in 1972; and, above all, addressing its operating deficits. The University had overextended itself financially during the 1960s, especially in granting tenure to unprecedented numbers of faculty. The recession and bear market triggered by the Iranian oil embargo of 1973 shrank Brown's chronically undersized endowment, raised operating costs, and brought matters to a crisis.

Donald F. Hornig, a former chemistry professor and acting

Donald F. Hornig, the fourteenth president of Brown, was a Harvard-trained chemist. As a member of the Manhattan Project in 1945, he was the last person to leave the Los Alamos, New Mexico, staging tower for the first atomic bomb prior to its detonation.

dean of the Graduate School who succeeded Ray Heffner as president in 1970, must have felt at times as if his appointment were a trial by fire. Under pressure to close a $4 million budget gap, the administration began admitting more undergraduates each year in order to collect more tuition and fees. It also began drawing on the endowment's capital to cover operating deficits. Unhappy with such emergency measures, Hornig asked the Corporation to name a committee on plans and resources, chaired by Thomas J. Watson Jr. '37, to devise long-term solutions to Brown's fiscal problems.

The Watson Report, released in 1974, recommended that Brown limit undergraduate enrollment to 5,150, seek a major increase in endowment as well as funds to implement the New Curriculum fully, cut back weaker departments and graduate programs, trim the number of tenured faculty, emphasize loans and work-study rather than outright scholarships in financial-aid packages, and move to year-round operation. The following February, Hornig issued a white paper based on the report; among other things, it recommended cuts in faculty positions and financial aid.

The plan alarmed and infuriated many segments of the Brown community, especially students. When their attempts to pressure the administration to adopt an alternate budget failed, nearly 3,000 undergraduates voted April 14 to go on strike. Many cut classes and picketed University Hall, but another referendum on April 22 failed to support a continued strike. Then, on April 23, the Corporation voted to approve the original budget. The next day, a group of forty students from the Third World Coalition took over University Hall and occupied it for two days, winning concessions on minority recruitment and support for the Afro-American studies program.

Protesting students marched around University Hall during the Third World Coalition's occupation of the building in April 1975.

But there was simply no getting around hard budgetary choices on financial aid and faculty cuts. Hornig had done what needed to be done, but he didn't enjoy the process or the backlash that it created. At the same time, Brown was facing a class-action lawsuit filed in 1974 by Assistant Professor of Anthropology Louise Lamphere after she was denied tenure. Lamphere's suit claimed that the University discriminated against women faculty in its hiring and promotion decisions. In July 1975, Hornig announced that he would step down the following summer, explaining that the retrenchment "has taken a toll on me and my family, as well as producing great strains on the fabric of the University."

The List Art Building opened in 1971.

The Hornig years weren't entirely a starvation diet for the University – Brown completed two major facilities, the Sciences Library and the List Art Center, and took over Bryant College's former campus on the East Side during that era – but the strains the president referred to were real. It remained for his successor to repair them while completing the financial retrenchment Hornig had begun – a tough balancing act. The Corporation searched long and thoughtfully before choosing Howard R. Swearer, the forty-four-year-old president of Carleton College in Minnesota, to take over the presidency at this difficult juncture.

Swearer, a native of Kansas who held a doctorate in political science from Harvard and had worked for the Ford Foundation, brought to the presidency an unpretentious Midwestern style and an ability to listen that soothed many anxieties and bruises. His low-key persona belied a decisiveness that had Brown operating in the black within eighteen months of his inauguration in 1977 – a balanced-budget commitment that has continued unbroken ever since. His confidence led him to launch a five-year, $158 million capital campaign in 1979. That goal was a stratospheric amount for Brown, and few believed the University would succeed. But as the *Providence Journal* described the out-

Howard R. Swearer, Brown's fifteenth president (1977–88), is credited with stemming the flow of red ink and putting Brown on a firm financial footing.

come: "Swearer, the son of a wildcat oil man who never made the big strike, helped bring in a gusher for Brown: more than $180 million." Annual giving also quadrupled during the Swearer years, and external funding for research more than tripled (from $13.2 million to $44.3 million), despite a decline in government support for universities. In 1983 the faculty awarded Swearer its highest honor, the Rosenberger Medal, citing "the abundant feeling of security you have rekindled in all of us."

Swearer's confidence was infectious, and it gave Brown a welcome boost in more than just its finances. Bronson's observation about President Andrews – "at his touch the old college leaped into new life and began to grow at an astonishing rate" – could also have been made about Howard Swearer. New programs and institutes, many of them interdisciplinary (as the architects of the New Curriculum had hoped), blossomed during his tenure: the A. Alfred Taubman Center for Public Policy and American Institutions, the Institute (later the Watson Institute) for International Studies, the Center

Students pass through the lobby of the five-story Center for Information Technology, the hub of Brown's computer facilities and instruction. The building was opened in 1988.

for Foreign Policy Development, the Center for Environmental Studies, and the Center for Old World Archaeology and Art, to name a few. Important new facilities were added, including the Geology-Chemistry Building and the Thomas J. Watson Sr. Center for Information Technology, which brought most of Brown's impressive computing resources and its computer science department under one roof.

Brown's curriculum had already outlived a decade of countervailing trends in higher education, during which most colleges that had dabbled in flexibility returned to conventional curricula. Yet Brown reflected what many saw as a larger trend toward the integration of knowledge – which was both a reaction against excessive intellectual specialization and fragmentation, and a desire for a new synthesis of all the knowledge born of this century's "information explosion." In the late 1970s, the curriculum's potential to reshape the entire academic enterprise at Brown finally became a reality, thanks in large part to a dynamic dean of the College, Walter Massey, who committed his office's resources to long-overdue curricular development and funding.

Modes of Thought courses had withered away through insufficient support, but the principle of integrative learning had taken hold and found expression in other ways. Under umbrellas such as Special Themes and Topics and Modes of Analysis, interdisciplinary perspectives were woven into the curriculum, spawning dozens of new concentration programs and revamping departmental offerings. Freed from distribution requirements, which tended to reinforce traditional disciplinary boundaries and produce standardized courses, faculty were encouraged to exercise more creativity and originality in their teaching.

An influential dean of the College from 1975 to 1979, physicist Walter Massey went on to become director of the National Science Foundation and later president of Morehouse College.

Students themselves demanded as much. No longer relegated to a passive role, they were eager to team up with faculty as partners in learning and to make their own contributions to research and teaching. The UTRA program (Undergraduate Teaching and Research Assistantships), launched in the 1980s by a Ford Foundation grant, became one of the most innovative and durable avenues for faculty-student collaboration. Based on a pilot program at Brown called Odyssey, it enabled students to work one-on-one with faculty to develop new ideas and approaches in scholarship and teaching – and the impetus for any given project could come from either a professor or a student. The success of UTRA/Odyssey illustrated the

THOMAS J. WATSON JR.
CLASS OF 1937

Thomas J. Watson Jr., class of 1937, son of the founder of IBM, was an indifferent student at Brown who almost became a commercial pilot after serving in the Army Air Corps in World War II. When he did decide to join his father's firm after the war, he proved to have the brains, the drive, and the foresight to help IBM create, and then dominate, the computer age. Where Watson Sr. was reluctant to give up punch cards (IBM's stock in trade), Watson Jr. saw the potential of electronic circuits, and later of magnetic tape and transistors. But he also knew that IBM's preeminence all along had been based on his father's principle of "systems knowledge" – customer service and technical support. From that foundation he built one of the most phenomenally successful companies in the world and helped launch a technological revolution. In 1957 Brown awarded him an honorary degree, and in 1968 he received the Rosenberger Medal. After retiring from IBM he served as ambassador to Moscow from 1979 to 1981 – coming full circle from World War II, when he had ferried Lend-Lease planes to the Red Army in Siberia. In 1991, Brown named its Institute for International Studies in his honor. Watson died on New Year's Eve, 1993, at the age of 79. In addition to the Watson Institute, his Brown legacies include the Arnold Fellowships for graduating seniors, Wriston faculty fellowships for curricular innovation, an endowed chair held by Nobel-winning physicist Leon Cooper, and a lifetime of gifts – most of them anonymous – in the vicinity of $50 million.

revitalizing effects of the curriculum, which were already obvious to anyone close to Brown. At a 1979 Commencement forum marking the curriculum's tenth anniversary, Chancellor Richard Salomon '32 rose from the audience to testify "on behalf of what the curriculum has done for Brown. We've made the greatest strides in the University's history by enacting it and sticking to it."

Brown's growing reputation seemed to validate Salomon's remark and helped answer the curriculum's perennial critics, who generally assumed that it fostered laziness. (Howard Swearer also took away some of their ammunition by persuading the fac-

Engineering professor Barrett Hazeltine was given a teaching-excellence award so many times by seniors at Commencement, it was renamed in his honor.

ulty to increase the number of course credits required for graduation, from 28 to 30.) Applications for admission to the College began to rise in the early 1980s, until by 1984–85 Brown had the largest applicant pool in the Ivy League – which meant that the caliber of students it admitted was higher than ever. In 1986 Swearer was named in a survey as one of the nation's ten most effective college presidents, and in 1987 *U.S. News and World Report* ranked Brown (for the first time) among the top ten major universities in the country.

Howard Swearer had come to Providence with his own vision of what he wanted to accomplish as a university president. A former acting director of UCLA's Russian and East European Studies Center and regional director of Peace Corps training programs, he was deeply interested in international relations and public service, two areas that thrived in Brown soil. The "inter-

Howard Swearer's emphasis on civic responsibility culminated in the establishment of Brown's Center for Public Service (renamed in Swearer's honor in 1991). By the end of the century, more than 1,400 students were contributing some 77,000 hours of service to the community each year

nationalization" of Brown began with the formation in 1979 of the Council for International Studies, superseded in 1986 by the Institute for International Studies – the brainchild of Swearer and Thomas J. Watson Jr. '37, former U.S. ambassador to the Soviet Union, for whom it was renamed in 1991. The Institute quickly became a leading think tank on international affairs, with a number of satellite programs and centers: the Center for Foreign Policy Development, the Population Studies and Training Center, and the Center for the Comparative Study of Development. Programs for international study expanded as well: by the late 1980s, Brown had more than 30 formal exchange agreements with foreign universities.

Swearer believed strongly that the academy and its members – faculty, staff, and students – had a responsibility to become involved with and to serve their communities in direct, tangible ways. He made Brown the headquarters of the Campus Com-

One of Brown's most fruitful and congenial partnerships was that of President Swearer and Artemis A.W. Joukowsky '55, a philanthropist who became a University trustee in 1985, vice chancellor in 1988, and chancellor in 1997.

pact, a coalition of more than 200 colleges and universities committed to integrating civic responsibility and higher education. The C.V. Starr National Fellowship Program, launched in 1981, endowed $1,000 scholarships for Brown students who delayed matriculation or took a leave of absence to work on public service projects. The Center for Public Service, founded in 1986 and renamed for Howard Swearer in 1991, became the campus clearinghouse for community-service and national-service projects, matching students with volunteer opportunities and helping them link those learning experiences to their academic studies. Swearer also served as president of the Rhode Island Public Expenditure Council and chaired a governor's commission studying state and local taxation – launching what came to be known as "the era of the external president."

Swearer's administration had its share of frustrations as well.

They included an unsuccessful attempt to revive ROTC, occa-sional run-ins with fraternities over unruly behavior, increased tensions between minority and white students, and growing stu-dent activism on issues such as free speech and Brown's invest-ment policies. (A group of students stood up and recited the poem "Jabberwocky" in the midst of a speech by CIA Director William Casey in 1981; CIA recruiters were interfered with in 1984; and in 1987, members of Students Against Apartheid dis-rupted a Corporation meeting.) Swearer also inherited the bur-den of implementing the Lamphere consent decree. Fashioned by U.S. District Court Judge Raymond Pettine as part of Brown's out-of-court settlement of the class-action suit in 1977, it granted tenure to Louise Lamphere and cash settlements to three other women faculty members, created an Affirmative Action Monitoring Committee, and required that all depart-ments develop goals and timetables for hiring women faculty.

Another source of controversy was the restaffing plan devel-oped in 1985 by Provost Maurice Glicksman, which recom-mended that Brown focus on its strengths instead of trying to be all things to all people. It proposed to shrink certain depart-ments, expand others, and shift a number of faculty to interdisci-plinary centers and programs. The plan ruffled some professorial feathers, especially among social-sciences faculty, who felt their departments were being undermined by the unchecked growth of interdisciplinary programs. Yet it represented, like the Wat-son Report a decade earlier, an ongoing effort by Brown to adopt the essential discipline of long-range, institution-wide strategic planning. As a result, when Swearer stepped down in 1989 to become director of Brown's Institute for International Studies, he left the University on a far more solid footing than he found it – and in a position to attract the most highly qualified candidate to succeed him as president.

*Chancellor Alva O. Way '51 (right)
introduces Vartan Gregorian as Brown's
sixteenth president in late August, 1988.*

7 | *Toward the New Millennium*

In light of Brown's growing internationalism, it was fitting that its next president would be a naturalized U.S. citizen. Vartan Gregorian, born in Iran of Armenian parents, was educated at the Collège Armenien in Beirut before winning a scholarship at Stanford, where he earned both a B.A. and a Ph.D. in history. He went on to teach at San Francisco State, the University of Texas at Austin, and the University of Pennsylvania, where he was named provost. In 1981 Gregorian accepted the job that made him famous: president of the New York Public Library. The once-great institution had been all but abandoned by its constituency and was in a state of decline when Gregorian took over. Within eight years he achieved a stunning turnaround, rallying New Yorkers – from the wealthy and influential to ordinary citizens – to support one of their foremost intellectual and cultural resources.

By the time he came to Brown, in January 1989, Gregorian had a reputation as something of a miracle worker, particularly in fund-raising. While Brown was in far better shape when Gregorian took the helm than the Public Library had been, and its endowment was no longer perilously low, its fiscal challenges nevertheless were considerable. The years since the previous capital campaign had been a period of such rapid expansion – both academically and physically – that the University's ambitions needed to be brought into balance with its resources once again.

One of the first things Gregorian did was put a temporary hold on the creation of new academic centers and interdepartmental programs (which it was generally agreed had reached critical mass) while he launched a review of existing programs. He also asked Dean of the College Sheila Blumstein to undertake a thorough evaluation of Brown's curriculum, then 20 years old and relatively unchanged since its inception, to make sure that (in his words) "it delivered what it promised." In 1987 the University had commissioned public-opinion researcher Daniel Yankelovich to survey graduates of the New Curriculum era – 1973 through 1985. The extensive survey found that Brown alumni overwhelmingly endorsed the curriculum, while at the same time they felt students would benefit from stronger advising and other support services. The Yankelovich survey's findings became a point of departure for Blumstein's internal review, which resulted in the development of a systematic Curricular Advising Program and the publication of a guidebook and workbook for incoming students to help them structure their Brown education.

The Guide to Liberal Learning identified several hundred existing courses that would serve as building blocks for a liberal education. It revived the title "University Courses" for such offerings, since they tended to be interdisciplinary in nature. Brown continued to impose no distribution requirements, but even before Gregorian's arrival, the University had begun requiring students to demonstrate writing competency in order to graduate, and it had created resources, such as the Rose Writing Fellows program, to help students polish their skills.

Near the end of his first year as president, Gregorian wrote an essay for Brown's annual report that sounded what would be the three dominant themes of his administration. Expanding the University's financial-aid resources topped his list of concerns. The cost of a Brown education, like the costs at most private colleges and universities, had risen faster than the average rate of inflation since the 1970s, putting such an education increasingly out of reach for middle-income families. Those at the lower end of the economic scale were in a better position to qualify for the limited amount of scholarship funding available; those in the middle were being squeezed hardest, with middle-income parents

Historian Carolyn Dean and anthropologist David Kertzer '69 were among the faculty stars hired during the Gregorian presidency.

and students being asked to assume the largest burden of debt.

Access to higher education, with all it implies about equality of opportunity, had become an increasingly contentious issue nationwide – but especially at elite, high-tuition private schools like Brown that were not rich enough to meet the financial-aid needs of every qualified student who applied for admission. Recognizing that Brown's excellence depended on its ability to attract and compete for the best students from all backgrounds, Gregorian wrote in his report: "Brown...has a particular responsibility to respond to the needs of [this country's] brightest children, regardless of color, creed, or financial circumstances....[W]e must find the resources to offer financial aid to all who qualify."

Gregorian's second major theme – recruiting the best new faculty in an increasingly competitive academic market – was equally central to his vision for Brown. As a former professor, Gregorian was committed to enhancing Brown's excellence in teaching and scholarship. As a first step, he announced a plan to endow a number of assistant professorships, something Brown (and most universities) had never done before. The University already had a reputation for hiring carefully at the junior faculty level and treating assistant professors not as temporary help, but

Afer Brown was founded in 1764, more than a century passed before it graduated anyone who was not a white male. The College took its first step toward racial diversity in 1877, when two African-American men – Inman Page and George Washington Milford – received bachelor's degrees. In 1891, the first two women – Mary Emma Woolley and Anne Tillinghast Weeden – enrolled, graduating in 1894 from what was to become the Women's College in Brown University, later renamed Pembroke College.

While only a handful of African Americans received Brown degrees before 1900, their later influence was substantial. Between 1877 and 1912, Brown graduated five black men who went on to become college presidents. The first African American to receive a graduate degree from Brown was John Wesley Gilbert, class of 1888, who earned his master's in 1891 and later taught at Paine Institute. Biologist Samuel M. Nabrit '32 Ph.D. was the first black man to earn a doctorate at Brown; he went on to teach at Morehouse College and later became president of Texas Southern University, as well as Brown's first black trustee. Among early graduates of the Women's College were two African-American sisters, Ethel Robinson '05 and Cora Robinson '09, both of whom became college teachers.

At the same time that blacks were beginning to attend Brown in small numbers, so too were Asians and, somewhat later, Asian Americans. The first

Graduate School pioneers: Julius Kumpei Matsumoto (top) of Japan received a master's degree in 1894. Samuel M. Nabrit '32 Ph.D. (above), a biologist, was the first black man to earn a Brown doctorate.

known Asian student to enroll at Brown was Sau-Ahbrah of Burma, class of 1877, who later earned his M.D. at Jefferson Medical College. Several students came to Brown before 1900 from Japan: Heita Okada, class of 1895; Julius Kumpei Matsumoto, who received a master's degree in 1894; and his brother,

Matsuzo Matsumoto, class of 1894. The first Korean student at Brown was Sang-Kyu Pack, class of 1905. Chinese students began arriving in small but regular numbers in 1906. John F. Aiso '31, the son of Japanese immigrants in California, was the first in a slow but steady trickle of Asian-American matriculants.

In 1955, a Brown chapter of the NAACP was founded. Well into the mid-1960s, however, the numbers of blacks on campus remained small. In December 1968, 65 of Brown's 85 African-American students walked down College Hill and camped in the Congdon Street Baptist Church for three days, asking that Brown increase the number of blacks in each entering class to 11 percent. The University agreed to fund minority recruitment and scholarship initiatives, and the next entering class included 128 new black students.

Today, Brown attracts (in roughly equal numbers) men and women from all 50 states and at least as many foreign countries. Approximately 10 percent of its undergraduates are international students, and more than one in four is a person of color. In 1999–2000, 15 percent of Brown's undergraduates were Asian American, 6 percent were African American, and 6 percent were Hispanic American.

Myra Liwanag '91 (top), of Filipino descent, was active at Brown as a minority peer counselor. In recent decades many African-American graduates (above) have worn colorful African sashes over their Commencement robes.

The Brown Daily Herald *comic strip* Thatch, *by Jeff Shesol '91, drew nationwide attention for affectionately skewering student life at the turn of the decade.*

as an investment in Brown's future. Adding endowed positions would make Brown even more attractive in the bidding wars for the best candidates.

Gregorian's third theme was that a world-class university demanded world-class libraries, laboratories, classrooms, and other facilities. As the first step in updating Brown's facilities, he vowed to tackle the physical plant's $50 million "deferred-maintenance" backlog.

The common thread linking all these concerns was a need for money – large sums of it. Gregorian noted in his essay that "Brown has a history, born out of necessity, of doing more with less," and he vowed to maintain fiscal responsibility while seeking the resources to meet these priorities. The obvious inference was that Brown would have to embark before long on another fund-raising campaign. But the time wasn't ripe yet; by early 1990, the nation's economy was decelerating and a recession was clearly around the corner.

In the meantime, Gregorian deployed his staff to find more efficient ways to operate. Fiscal restraint enabled Brown to reduce its annual rate of increasing tuition and fees to less than 5 percent and to index the financial aid budget to the annual tuition increase for the first time, guaranteeing that the two would always rise proportionately. Endowment spending was reduced as well, to just over 4 percent annually. The University prioritized deferred maintenance needs so that the most urgent could be tackled right away. Academic and fiscal planning, previously semi-autonomous processes, became more integrated, taking Brown to a new level of strategic change.

Gregorian had other goals that extended beyond Brown. To increase diversity in higher education – particularly at the faculty and administrative levels – he created the Leadership Alliance, a coalition of colleges and universities committed to increasing the flow of talented minority students through high school, college, and graduate school, and into academia. But diversity, already a source of occasional tension on campus, became a critical issue early in Gregorian's tenure, and it forced this most accessible and public of Brown presidents into the national limelight under circumstances he hardly would have chosen. Within months of his inauguration, a flurry of racist incidents directed at minority students (name-calling, anonymous notes, and the like) had the campus in an uproar and Brown in the news. Gregorian made his views explicit at a rally on the Green, where he said: "There are many outlets in this nation for racism, bigotry, and dehumanization. Brown will not be one of them, I assure you." Not long afterward, the University enacted an anti-harassment behavior code.

At the same time, Gregorian bucked the trend of "political correctness" to keep the Brown community hospitable to a wide range of views. He brought distinguished speakers of every political stripe to campus, from sixties radical Angela Davis to conservative Supreme Court Justice Antonin Scalia, and created the President's Lecture Series in 1992 to ensure a steady flow of diverse ideas and intellectual debate. Gregorian spoke out frequently and forcefully in defense of intellectual freedom, and he prided himself on the fact that during his tenure no speech, however controversial, was cut short by protest.

He had less luck, however, keeping the University's daily business from being disrupted. In the spring of 1992, a group of 250 students occupied University Hall during a daylong protest over financial aid. When, after repeated warnings, the protestors would not leave the building, they were arrested (they later pleaded no contest and agreed to pay court costs). The protest was partially a consequence of a national economic downturn, which saw many students' economic circumstances change for the worse.

Among the institution-wide cuts required to balance the budget that year were funding for four varsity sports: women's volleyball and gymnastics, and men's golf and water polo. Those cuts, in turn, triggered a Title IX-based lawsuit that charged Brown with discriminating against women athletes. Ironically, a preliminary injunction against Brown was granted in 1992 by the same Judge Raymond Pettine who had fashioned the Lamphere consent decree – and who had just agreed to vacate the decree after 15 years, a period in which the number of tenured women faculty quintupled. Pettine later ruled against Brown on Title IX, and the case failed the appeals process; the two women's teams were restored to varsity status, and Brown was ordered by the courts to achieve parity in varsity sports opportunities for men and women. The 1991–92 academic year also saw Howard Swearer's untimely death from cancer, at the age of 59.

The following spring, amid signs that the national recession had bottomed out, Gregorian decided the time had come to launch a major fund-raising campaign. In April 1993 he announced a $450 million, five-year "Campaign for the Rising Generation" – by far the most ambitious in Brown's history. Its goal was nothing less than the reendowment of the University on all levels: faculty, undergraduate and graduate programs, library, facilities, financial-aid budget, endowment, and physical plant.

The campaign aimed high and came in even higher – a total of $534 million – doubling Brown's total endowment to more

At a financial-aid fund-raising gala held in New York's Grand Central Station in 1994, President Gregorian greeted friends such as Brown parent Carly Simon.

than $800 million. Its success brought the University within reach of many of its long-range goals and enabled it to launch major new initiatives. The campaign endowed 43 new faculty chairs, 27 for senior professors and 16 for assistant professors; raised $40 million for undergraduate scholarships and $16 million for graduate fellowships; increased funding for the library system by $23 million; established special programs, such as the Royce Fellowships for outstanding undergraduates and the Salomon Research Awards for faculty; and provided funds to renovate existing buildings and construct new ones (including MacMillan Hall, an undergraduate sciences center). At the same time, the University recognized that some of its key priorities would be achieved only incrementally, not instantly by this or any other fund-raising effort. For example, although the undergraduate scholarship endowment doubled, Gregorian acknowledged that the ideal of truly need-blind admissions would require at least three times that amount.

The campaign brought in a number of large gifts, including the historic Nightingale-Brown House on Benefit Street given to the University by the Brown family to serve as the John Nicholas Brown Center for the Study of American Civilization. The largest single windfall was Ambassador Walter Annenberg's 1993 gift of $50 million to endow the National Institute for School Reform (later renamed the Annenberg Institute) at Brown. Awarded as part of his unprecedented $500 million "Challenge to the Nation" grant to stimulate education-reform initiatives, Annenberg's gift to Brown recognized the University's leadership in school reform beginning in the mid-1980s, when it had recruited Theodore Sizer to head its education department and had given a home to his new Coalition of Essential Schools.

Six months after the campaign's successful conclusion, and eight years after he was sworn in as president, Gregorian announced he would leave Brown in July 1997 and return to New York to head the Carnegie Corporation. He had done his part for Brown, Gregorian believed, and now it was time to move on to his next challenge. Professor Sizer, in an interview with the *Providence Journal*, summed up the Gregorian era by observing that the litmus test of a college president is the quality of faculty brought in during his tenure. "There has been a string of brilliant appointments of rising young faculty," Sizer told the *Journal*. "That's even more important than the extraordinary campaign for funds."

In a "State of the University" speech to a special convocation in March 1997, Gregorian cited the many other strides Brown had made in eight years. In addition to 270 new faculty hired, 72 senior professors had been appointed to endowed chairs. Applications to the College had reached a record of more than 15,000 for the class of 2000 (making Brown one of the half-dozen most selective schools in the United States). In that same class, the percentage of students receiving scholarship aid from Brown – 38 percent – reached an all-time high. The library had grown from two million to three million volumes, and was rapidly transforming itself through information technology; users could now access the entire system through its on-line catalog, JOSIAH. Eleven of Brown's strongest academic programs (including neurosciences and American civilization) had been elevated to departmental rank. Community ties and collaborative projects multiplied through the efforts of Brown's public-service programs and its new Office of Government and Community Relations. And Brown had maintained its identity as a community while becoming more diverse, in every sense of the word: the proportion of minority students rose from 21 to 29 percent, the number of international students increased 17 percent, and the number of women faculty increased 40 percent.

But as he prepared to leave Brown, Gregorian placed just as much emphasis on what remained to be done as he did on what had been accomplished. Under his direction, strategic plans for the coming decades were developed by six task forces focusing on the Graduate School, liberal education in the 21st century, academic resources, information resources, business and administrative operations, and the University's mission statement. Other works in progress included renovating Carr House to serve as the English department's new headquarters, constructing a new home for the Watson Institute for International Studies, and launching a major fund-raising campaign for the School of Medicine. And, of course, finding a successor to lead Brown – now nearly two and half centuries old, and more vital than ever – into the 21st century. Gregorian concluded his "State of the University" speech by paraphrasing Thomas Wolfe on America: "I think the true fulfillment of Brown's role in higher education is yet to come. I think the true discovery of Brown's potential is still before us, I think the true appreciation of a liberal education is before us, and I think that all these things are certain, as certain as the morning, as inevitable as noon."

An extroverted leader, Gordon Gee brought Brown's presidency into the Ratty and the residence halls, where students responded enthusiastically to his energy and wit.

8 | *New Horizons*

As if to challenge the certainties invoked in Gregorian's last major address as president, the next two years saw the University undergo a series of rapid changes – with an unexpected twist.

In late June 1997, the Corporation announced that it had chosen E. Gordon Gee, a 53-year-old Utah-born Mormon who had made state-university presidencies his career since the age of 37, to be Brown's 17th president. At the time, Gee was in his fifth year as president of the Ohio State University, where he had distinguished himself as a consummate politician and fund-raiser while effecting a brisk sequence of controversial academic cutbacks that had stabilized Ohio State's gargantuan operating budget. With his rapid-fire Midwestern patter, colorful bow ties, and lack of a traditional academic background (he has a J.D. and an Ed.D., both from Columbia, but no Ph.D.), Gee represented a 180-degree stylistic departure from his scholarly Brown predecessors. Students, colleagues, and alumni were charmed by their energetic new leader, on the whole, but some members of the faculty received Gee more skeptically – a reaction that may have played a part in the surprising turn of events that transpired two years later.

Gee took office formally in January 1998 and immediately began mobilizing his senior leadership to undertake a University-wide process of self-evaluation and change, with a particular emphasis on strengthening the Graduate School. Work continued on the long-awaited external "cluster" reviews of academic disciplinary areas, whose findings would serve as a platform for future restructuring. An example of the sort of collaborative academic model Gee had in mind for graduate and faculty scholarship at

Brown was the Brain Sciences Program, which was inaugurated in the fall of 1999 and involved nearly 90 faculty from 10 separate departments and disciplines: cognitive and linguistic sciences, computer science, neuroscience, psychology, physics, psychiatry and human behavior, clinical neuroscience, and the divisions of applied mathematics, biology and medicine, and engineering.

In addition, at the May 1999 Commencement, Gee and Brown's chancellor, Stephen Robert '62, launched a far-reaching program to incorporate the study of values into numerous academic and civic endeavors on campus. The Stephen Robert Initiative for the Study of Values included undergraduate courses, colloquia for faculty and graduate students, and an annual symposium and lecture series open to the public – all aimed at examining "the elements of any good life: ethics and a just community, spirituality and beauty, friendship and love, physical well-being and freedom from fear."

Neuroscience professor John Donoghue was a founding academic leader of Brown's Brain Sciences Program, established in the fall of 1999.

Meanwhile, the physical plant was growing again. In October 1998, Brown unveiled a new state-of-the-art science facility, W. Duncan MacMillan Hall, named to honor the contributions of the longtime trustee ('53) and located on the corner of Thayer and George streets. The century-old Ladd Observatory, which stands a mile north of the campus on the highest point in Providence, reopened its doors for student star-gazing and neighborhood gatherings after extensive repairs and renovations. Work commenced on the transformation of the former Carr's Restaurant on Angell Street

The Watson Institute for International Studies brought prominent speakers to campus, including former Secretary of State Robert McNamara, a key strategist during the Vietnam War.

into a new home for the English department, as well as on a major renovation and addition to the engineering and physics building. Ground was broken in 1999 for a new home for the Watson Institute for International Studies closer to the main campus, on Thayer Street, and the administration began to move forward with plans for a new life-sciences building adjacent to the biomedical center on Meeting Street. In addition, the conversion of the former Sayles Gymnasium on the Pembroke Campus into a classroom facility was nearly complete by the time Brown entered the new millennium.

Keeping pace with the optimism of a remarkably robust U.S. economy, the College's popularity continued to swell. The admission office received a record number of applications for the class of 2004 (some 16,500) – helped, perhaps, by a more generous financial-aid policy implemented under Gee's leadership the previous spring. Turning to the quality of undergraduate life at Brown, in late 1999 Gee appointed Brown's first vice president for campus life and student services, Princeton dean of students Janina Montero. "Brown will be ready for the coming year, the next decade, and the next century," Gee wrote in his introduction to the annual financial report published just before the new year. But few were ready for what happened shortly thereafter.

*In the wake of President Gee's resigna-
tion, two women led the University:
Interim President Sheila Blumstein
(above), and Executive Vice President
and Provost Kathryn Spoehr (right).*

On February 6, 2000, Chancellor Robert informed senior
administrators that after two years as Brown's president, Gordon
Gee had accepted an offer to become chancellor of Vanderbilt
University. The news, so totally unexpected, shocked the Brown
community. While Gee's Vanderbilt salary would place him
among the highest-paid university leaders in the country, foremost among his stated reasons for leaving was what he described
as a poor "fit" between him and Brown.

Within two days, the Corporation appointed former dean of
the College (and former interim provost) Sheila Blumstein, a
professor of cognitive and linguistic sciences, to serve as Brown's
interim president while a search committee was formed to hire
Gee's successor. The swift appointment of Blumstein, an admired
administrator and distinguished faculty member for 30 years,
was unanimously well received on campus. In addition, Brown's
provost, Kathryn Troyer Spoehr '69, a cognitive scientist and

former dean of the Graduate School and of the faculty, reassured her colleagues at an emergency meeting that Brown could withstand even the most abrupt change of leadership. Since joining the faculty in 1974, she reminded them, she had seen four presidents come and go. "Frankly," she said, as her colleagues rose to applaud, "what has happened [this week] doesn't faze me in the least."

Just as it had in the late 1960s, Brown University had once again pulled itself together after an unusually short presidential tenure. But much more so than in the wake of Ray Heffner's term, Brown in the year 2000 was on possibly the firmest institutional footing of its 236 years. With one of the most highly qualified undergraduate student bodies in the Ivy League, a distinguished faculty committed to innovative scholarship, a Medical School celebrating 25 years of health-care leadership in the state and the region, and a Graduate School poised for new initiatives and excellence, Brown stood more than ready to welcome its 18th president, a leader with whom it could reach new heights in the 21st century.

❦ Bibliography

Barry, Jay, and Martha Mitchell. *A Tale of Two Centuries*. Providence: Brown Alumni Monthly, 1985.

Bronson, Walter C. *The History of Brown University, 1764–1914*. Providence: Brown University, 1914.

Boucher, Norman. "A Week in February." *Brown Alumni Magazine*, vol. 100, no. 4, March-April 2000.

Crane, Theodore R. "Four Presidents and Their Roles in Educational Renewal during Brown's History." *Brown Alumni Monthly*, vol. 76, no. 1, September 1975, pp. 18-24.

Cremin, Lawrence A. *American Education: The Colonial Experience, 1607–1783*. New York: Harper & Row, 1970.

Diffily, Anne. "One Hundred Years of Women at Brown." *Brown Alumni Monthly*, vol. 92, no. 4, December 1991–January 1992.

Diffily, Anne. "Hello, College Hill." *Brown Alumni Magazine*, vol. 98, no. 2, November-December 1997.

Hofstadter, Richard. *Anti-Intellectualism in American Life*. New York: Vintage Books, 1963.

Kaufman, Polly Welts, ed. *The Search for Equity: Women at Brown University, 1891–1991*. Providence: Brown University Press, 1991.

Mitchell, Martha. *Encyclopedia Brunoniana*. Providence: Brown University Library, 1993.

McLoughlin, William G. *Rhode Island: A History*. New York: W.W. Norton & Company/Nashville: American Association for State and Local History, 1978.

Phillips, Janet. "Carpe Diem: Twenty-Five Years of (R)evolution." *Brown Alumni Monthly*, vol. 95, no. 6, March 1995.

Providence Journal-Bulletin. Article on Vartan Gregorian's resignation, January 7, 1997.

Providence Sunday Journal. Obituary of Howard Swearer, Oct. 20, 1991.